It
Was
FUN!

It
Was
FUN!

BEVERLY NICHOLSON

authorHOUSE®

AuthorHouse™
1663 Liberty Drive
Bloomington, IN 47403
www.authorhouse.com
Phone: 1-800-839-8640

First published by AuthorHouse   09/19/2011

ISBN: 978-1-4634-4188-3 (sc)
ISBN: 978-1-4634-4189-0 (hc)
ISBN: 978-1-4634-4190-6 (ebk)

Library of Congress Control Number: 2011913153

Printed in the United States of America

ACKNOWLEDGEMENTS

THIS BOOK WOULD NOT HAVE BEEN COMPLETED WITHOUT THE WISDOM AND EXPERIENCE OF OUR FRIEND KATIE WATSON. SHE GAVE MANY WISE SUGGESTIONS (AND ENCOURAGEMENTS) THAT WERE INVALUABLE.

DIGITAL PROFESSIONALS LENT MUCH NEEDED HELP IN THE SCANNING AND PRINTING PROCESS.

FRIENDS AND FAMILY WERE VERY SUPPORTIVE DURING THIS TIME. THANKS TO ALL OF YOU! A SPECIAL THANKS, TO THE FRIENDS AND FAMILY WHO TOOK TIME TO WRITE LETTERS FOR THE EPILOGUE.

NICK AND I ESPECIALLY WANT TO ACKNOWLEDGE OUR APPRECIATION TO NOTED ARTIST AND CARICATURIST DANNY PICINI OF CRANSTON, R I, FOR DONATING HIS TIME AND TALENT IN PROVIDING THE CARICATURE OF NICK IN THE EPILOGUE.

AS IN NEARLY ALL OF OUR PROJECTS OVER THE YEARS, NICK PROVIDED NEEDED AND TIMELY ASSISTANCE IN THIS ENDEAVOR AS WELL.

INTRODUCTION

Morris Eugene "Nick" Nicholson has an interesting combination of personality traits. He can be very tough at work, but tender and compassionate at home with the family. (Would you believe *I* was the disciplinarian at our house? This is not so surprising when you learn that his Mother enforced the rules. He is very frugal and drives a hard bargain in stores and on the job—but unbelievably generous with his family, church and friends.

People have asked me, "how do you live with this man?" half joking and half not. If we had met in an office setting we might not have married. We are too different businesswise.

His faith is the cornerstone of his life. He's also a helper. If a friend or family member is in need they know where to look. Nick will be there for them.

He carefully prepares for everything. His mantra: "always find the best way and then do it that way." I once gave him a pillow saying, "I'm not bossy, I just have better ideas." Right.

I have always told Nick, "you are so resourceful!" One day we were on our way to a meeting and discovered we had forgotten an essential telephone number. I would have returned home to retrieve it. Nick suggested, "let's call Melva, she will have the number." She did. No time lost. He has shown this same resourcefulness in many other instances over the years.

Nick has always felt the need to prove 'he's the best.' This need was probably formed in early childhood and further enhanced in the Marine Corps.

He so identifies with others he has a difficult time controlling his emotions. An example: when we lived in our first house, our neighbors the Farrars had two teenage daughters, Dottie and Diane. We were close with the family and to the intense sorrow of all who knew her, Dottie died at age 30. Nick completely broke down when he saw her in her casket.

He has an old fashioned work ethic, courtesy of his mom and the Corps. Some people have told me that he has the ability to make others feel important. I agree. To his friends and family he's a pussycat, but to business competitors he can be hard as nails. If you want to see how really quirky he is read chapter 8. I have been married to him for 52 plus years and I've seen lots of "quirky."

Let's hear it for Podunk, Texas!

The word "Podunk" lacks a certain something. It utterly fails to arouse in the human breast vistas of grandeur or far away exotic places. Ah, but if you grew up in "Podunk" now that's another matter!

Yes, Virginia, there really is a Podunk, in fact several of them. Nick grew up in Podunk, Texas, as opposed to Podunk, Ct., or any of the other four scattered across the country. How did I learn this earth shattering fact, you might ask? A book has now been written about the town of Podunk, Texas. (Take that New York!) Nick just recently discovered this book and read about people he had known during his school days. The general location of Podunk—also known as Denver Harbor Subdivision—is in east Houston.

Nick was so excited to discover this book, he was sharing information about it even to casual acquaintances. He took the book on recent our trip to Charlotte, NC, and was discussing the book with our son-in-law, Tony. (More information about our sweet Tony later in this book.) As he was telling the book title, "Where the Hell is Podunk, Texas?" He was suddenly aware that his 10 year old granddaughter was present. "Oh, Katy, I'm sorry that was a bad word!" Tony quickly said with mock seriousness, "yeah, Katy, I don't ever want to hear you say 'Podunk'!" That ended the discussion as everyone erupted in laughter. (More about Podunk later.)

TABLE OF CONTENTS

CHAPTER 1

HOW DID THIS WHOLE THING GET STARTED?

The big adventure almost ended before it began. Things started out well in December 1969. John McLeod a successful Dallas businessman, offered to financially help Nick and his partner Carl Jacobson, get started in business. The name "Apollo Paper Incorporated" was registered in Austin, an office secured, warehouse made ready, suppliers in place and a truck purchased. The plan was to open January 2, 1970. Then the hammer fell.

In mid-January Carl decided to return to his job rather than take the risk of starting a new business. He was hired back at Brawner by his boss, Joe Arnold. Carl had been a salesman at Brawner Paper Company for 20 years.

Nick and I were both in a state of shock. He started smoking again, we had extended prayer meetings and through it all we wondered: would John McLeod continue to support Apollo with only one person in charge instead of two? God mercifully intervened. After Carl returned to Brawner Joe Arnold called Nick. "You got the wrong guy. I'm ready to leave Brawner and Carl isn't."

Joe had been at Brawner for 19 years. He had an impressive resume. He had graduated from the University of Texas and played football with Darrell Royal. Following graduation he had been instrumental in setting up Brawner's computer program. Neither Carl nor Nick possessed any experience or even interest in this area. God knew what we needed better than we did.

After that harrowing beginning things proceeded in a much more calm and orderly manner. John McLeod of course was delighted at the way things had worked out. Joe set up office procedures and supervised payables and receivables. He coined a very wise saying in regard to receivables, "We solicit payment of your account in the same courteous manner we solicited your order."

Soon after the company opened the Dallas division was begun as well. In those first few months it was necessary for Nick and Joe to make the trips together. On one such trip after flying up, they had no ground transportation. John McLeod met them after work and gave them the use of his Cadillac.

As he got out of the car he flipped a switch that raised the steering wheel. Neither Nick nor Joe could figure out how to lower it again. Consequently Joe drove all over Dallas with the wheel in the "up" position. Poor country bumpkins!

Joe had a keen sense of humor. While Nick was on vacation one year Joe with some help, covered Nick's office with strings to look like cobwebs. There were pictures taken to commemorate the occasion and everyone enjoyed the joke.

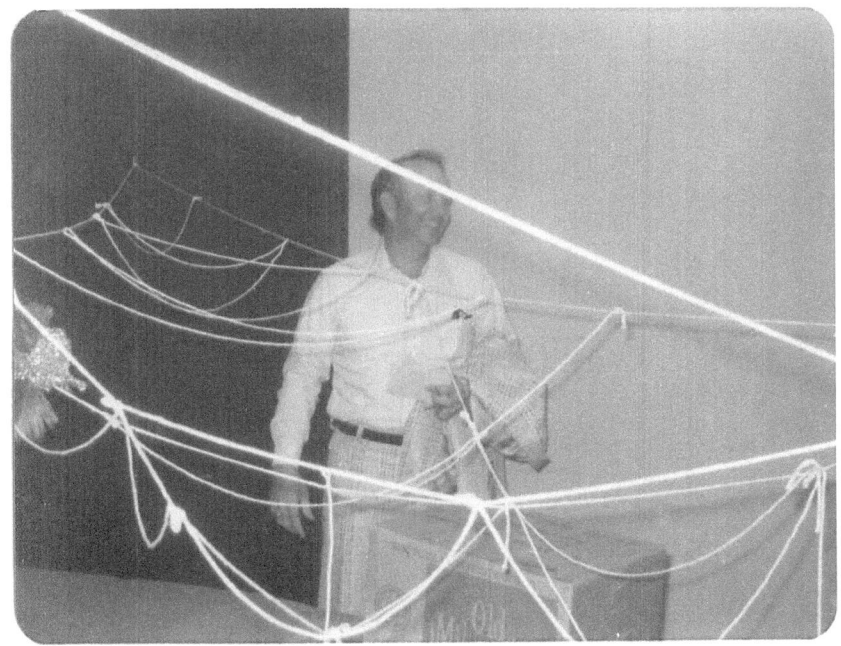

NICK'S NEWLY DECORATED OFFICE

When the company first started there were only a few chairs in the conference room. There was a need for a table. The warehouse guys had tried for 15-20 minutes to install a 15' one. Joe saw what was happening measured the table, had them back it up, turn it on its side and it slid right through the door. "You bunch of dummies!" laughed a bystander. "It's a good thing that Old gray-headed supervisor told you how to do it. You'd never have figured it out!" The name stuck and Joe was forever after, 'that old gray-headed supervisor.'

CONFERENCE ROOM. JOE IS ON THE RIGHT, NICK ON
THE LEFT AT THE HEAD OF THE TABLE.

It was decided that the company needed a logo on their business forms. Nick suggested Roland Rollins a company employee design them. (More about Roland later.) Joe said an artist who specialized in these forms should be used. Nick, ever watchful of company funds asked, "you mean *pay for it*?" "Yes." The plan was for the artist to submit three or four designs for their consideration. The chosen logo featured a red "space ship" (pictured as an elongated dot) launched against a background of blue. Since the space program had been the inspiration for the title "Apollo" they felt it continued the theme and carried out the idea of rapid growth, the message they wanted to convey.

Dan Drake was the founder and owner of Drake Container. Apollo was started in the back portion of Drake Container's warehouse. Nick and Dan were friends and had an ongoing debate about whose company had the "ugliest" logo. Dan said Apollo's logo looked like a .22 caliber bullet shot through a tin can. Nick retorted that Dan's "duck coming out of a box" had to be the worst!

APOLLO LOGO QUOTE BY DAN DRAKE:
"It looks like a .22 bullet shot through a tin can!"

Years later, sadly, Joe had a stroke. He was later to say he was dressing for work but unable to attach his tie tack. Following that he said everything went black. A few years later Joe died as a result.

Strike #1, strike #2—home run!

Those early years were not without their crises. A man brought suit against the company. He claimed to have received permanent injury from a product his company purchased from Nick and Joe. The suit was for two million dollars. Meanwhile, Nick and Joe's insurance company cancelled Apollo's coverage because they discovered the company sold bowl cleaner containing acid.

Apollo did not manufacture the product, however the claim was the drum was not labeled. Since he had no guidelines for its use Apollo was liable. In these inflated times two million sounds like a fairly small settlement. Back then it was an enormous amount and bankruptcy looked inevitable.

For days Nick, Joe and other employees went through records. It was necessary to recover evidence to prove they had logged in the chemical and it was properly labeled. Finally the receipt was found and the employee who had recorded it was set to testify in court.

A second shock was in store. The day before the trial was to begin the lawyer representing Apollo resigned from the bar! The judge granted them two weeks to find a new lawyer and prepare their defense. Enter John Boswell, a member of First Baptist church in Houston and a specialist in product liability. He crafted a brilliant defense in the short time allotted him and again we experienced the Lord's protection from certain disaster.

The infamous retailers' specialty company

Nick had cut his business teeth on his first company called Retailers' Specialty. He and John Byers his future business partner, met while working together at Pollock Paper Co as salesmen. Pollock assigned Nick territory out in the country selling mainly to mom and pop grocery stores. Nick drove a 1956 Ford with no air-conditioning clad in a suit and tie. He agreed to start in a country territory but requested a city territory when one became available. Six months later he got his opportunity. He was promised a commission if he made more than his "draw."

Doris Brown was just a rookie receptionist/switchboard operator when this story took place. She had just started with Industrial Insulators, one of the accounts Nick was assigned to call on for Pollock Paper. Doris was destined to work in related businesses for the next forty years; later attaining highly responsible positions.

It was Nick's first time to call on the company. "Hi, I'm Nick and I would like to see Jack Davis." She called Jack and announced him. "Who is he with?" "Oh, he's just by himself." It became a running joke between Nick and Doris over the years. She would ask, "are you still by yourself?" Always good for a laugh.

As he continued to call on accounts, he learned from a supplier how much money he made for Pollock just off this one particular account. Nick realized the costs were being inflated for the entire sales force! They did not intend to have to pay many bonuses! He confronted his boss Mr. Bloodworth, about this. His reply was, "it's out of my hands."

About this time John suggested he and Nick start their own company. Nick accepted. Retailers had a very humble beginning—a one room office and a 2000 square foot warehouse—on a dirt road in a tin building. This also began Nick's all-night trips to Emmitt Smiths' place of business in Liberty, Texas, to buy paper products. He would truck the load of paper back and sell it to various local customers. I asked him why he did this. He said Retailers' was too small to go through regular sources. He "bootlegged" paper from Emmitt, who could buy from large sources like International Paper. In this way Nick could buy cheaper and be more competitive.

He made the mistake of telling me he was expecting a large shipment from the Dura Lee Company, a supplier that sold printed bags for specific customers. This was a mistake because each day I would inquire if the shipment had arrived. In the following days and weeks, I was growing more angry each day that this company would treat my husband with such disrespect! The fact of the matter was: the shipment was never coming until he paid for the last order. Need I mention this operation was started on a shoe string?

Nick and John were often forced to go to banks, hat in hand to try to secure a loan. After one such appointment I asked if they had received any money. John replied, "no, but they kissed us!" Nick later observed that when capital was needed they couldn't get it. Years later after he no longer needed it, banks came to him seeking to lend! Fortunately months later they secured an SBA (small business) loan.

As things gradually improved Nick hired Ralph McSpadden and A.J. Courville as his first salesmen. Leon Jarmon became the new warehouse manager and Jane Mock handled office duties. Prior to that Jean, John's wife and I worked as office volunteers.

A.J. and Ralph proved to be organized and methodical. Leon was a ray of sunshine always upbeat and willing to do whatever. Jane, eighteen years old from Miles, Tx., made no secret that she loved cowboys. She too was an excellent employee. One of the things I remember about Jane was the time she was involved in a car accident. Disregarding any injury she might have had, she was searching frantically for her wig. The impact had knocked it off her head and into the back seat.

Jane's life was tragically cut short a few years later due to a botched cancer operation. She had made her peace with the Lord and eagerly told everyone of the change He made in her life. She told Nick, "I thought Jesus was far away but He was close by all the time."

After a few years sad to say, it became obvious John was an inept businessman and had resorted to dishonesty (with the help of Charles the company CPA) to gain control of Retailers'. Nick felt he had no choice but to leave the company and seek another situation.

Some would call the following scenario a coincidence but we know better. Just at the time this was happening at the company, our pastor at Westheimer Baptist Church preached a sermon entitled, "would a man rob God?" The subject was tithing. Following the service in the parking lot Nick was visibly shaken. "We have been robbing God" (by not tithing) he said with conviction. "We must start at once!" This could not have come at a worse time financially for our family, but we managed to tithe with God's help.

Exactly a year from that date, Nick was in the process of starting Apollo Paper. Coincidence? There are no coincidences in the Christian's life. Isaiah 66:2b, "but on this one I will look: on him who is poor and of a contrite spirit, and who trembles at My word."

CHAPTER 2

NICK: A STUDY IN CONTRASTS

Nick's formative years are a study in contrasts. Extreme contrasts. He was the youngest of five children, three older brothers and one sister.

Extreme alcoholism was one of the main influences in his life. His father (Paw Paw) drew a government check each month for a disability he suffered in WW 1. Nearly every cent went to support his habit. This caused the rest of Nick's family to scramble to pay the $33 a month house note and keep food on the table.

Although Nick's growing up years were greatly influenced by alcoholism, he also experienced extreme enjoyment. Have your jaws ever "locked" when you tasted food that was indescribably good? Neither have mine but Nick still experiences that sensation from time to time. (Not only have I not experienced it—I've never heard of anyone else who has either!) He tells of making the enjoyment of a dill pickle last all day because he didn't have a nickel to buy another one.

To this day he gets pleasure out of the simplest things. He enjoys yard work then sitting back in a lawn chair, watering it and admiring his work. He likes working until near exhaustion then waking up refreshed after a long nap or good night's sleep.

During his early teens he loved playing all kinds of team sports. He didn't discover golf until he was in his thirties. (Golf was not part of the Denver Harbor vocabulary.) Basketball and baseball were the sports he loved most. He was a skinny kid growing up. The first time he was tackled in football he knew this sport was not for him.

Mr. Carter who lived down the street, became a surrogate father. Another was Pop McCoy who lived across the street. Mr. Carter and Nick were drawn together by their mutual love for sports. Mr. Carter bought "The Sporting News" read it and passed it on to Nick. Their friendship was forever cemented when he bought Nick his first and only basketball. Each night it was carefully stored under his bed. It was his prize possession.

Excelling at sports filled a real need in Nick's life. He had "something to prove" as successful people often do. He used it as a statement to disprove, "he's just like his old man." These hurtful words would sometimes get back to him.

Although short (he grew six inches between junior high and high school) he developed a deadly long-range shot in basketball and pitched several no hitters in baseball. Nick paid for the latter in the long run by throwing curve balls long before his elbow was developed enough to handle it. The result—no Yankee pitching contract! Some dreams die hard.

Nick spent hours at Pop's house watching him sharpen saws and make fish (Gill) nets to sell. His son Johnny, took Nick fishing in nearby rivers and lakes. Nick loved to listen to the wisdom of both Mr. Carter and Pop McCoy. Of course they loved having such an interested listener as well.

He had his share of extreme disappointments too. Christmas actually to both of us, was not the happiest of holidays. Mine because I lived in an upper middle class neighborhood—and we were not. In school after Christmas I embellished the presents I had received. Mine never seemed to measure up to what others in the class received. Nick and his siblings received an apple and orange courtesy of the Dayton Fire Department in his early youth. This was prior to the move to Houston.

Another frustration was dropping out of all sports to take "Distributive Education." This was a high-sounding program for kids who needed to begin work at noon but qualified to receive credit for attending school all day.

He lost the title, "Best Dressed" in his senior year of high school. During elementary and junior high years he had two pairs of pants and two shirts to last for the entire school year. By his senior year he had saved enough money to buy some nice clothes. He longed for the recognition to help take the sting out of those early years. It was not to be. He came in second.

Speaking of the early years in 7th grade, "David" had the temerity to say, "here comes Morris in that same old plaid shirt and jeans he wears all the time!" A few bystanders found this amusing. Nick exacted revenge on David later that day on the playground.

"SHE COULD MOVE MORE DIRT WITH A TEASPOON
THAN MOST PEOPLE COULD WITH A BACKHOE"

Nick's first drill instructor—his Mom

Annie Beatrice Glass was 16 years old when she married Nick's father, Joseph Johnson Nicholson. From all accounts it was an arranged marriage. J.J. was twenty years her senior and a friend of her father's.

When Nick and I married I asked her if I could call her "Nanny" because that was what everyone called her. J.J. was always called "Paw Paw." No one knows what their early marriage was like but by the time the children started coming, Paw Paw was on his way to becoming an alcoholic.

Nanny's expectations of life were very modest. She had a servant's heart and was a kind, gentle person. This was the picture of their grandmother Mark and Lynda knew and loved. They were shocked to hear stories from Nick that presented a slightly different view of their beloved Nanny.

In her younger days Nanny was a stern disciplinarian. She had developed a "memorable switching" to an art form for those who didn't toe the mark. Also, pinching the offender in church with a vow to "just wait until you get home," struck terror in every heart. Nick and his sister the last two at home in those days would stay out of sight as much as possible after church. They would reappear at supper time hoping she had forgotten. To their dismay they would discover, sometimes even the next day, that she had not!

She was creative in her discipline. Nick and Ann were banished to the floor under their bed for a specified length of time. During these episodes, the conspirators planned elaborate mutinies that seldom if ever happened.

Hers was no life of leisure and luxury. Nick recalls that her hands were rough and broken from scrubbing clothes for seven people on a rub board. She was allotted $10.00 a week to feed the whole family. This was in earlier days when all the children were still at home. He remembers times he would awaken at 3:00am to find her ironing clothes for the next day. If it had rained she would iron all the clothes dry. Nanny would sometimes lie down for 30 minutes during the day from sheer exhaustion.

They had no car so Nick pulled a wagon to haul groceries home. They went to several stores buying only the specials. She would endure embarrassment if she miscalculated the total and had to put back an item or two but this seldom happened because she kept an accurate running total in her head.

Many nights Paw Paw came home brandishing a gun and threatening everyone in the house. On these nights, Nan would endure mental and physical abuse without complaint. The following day she patiently mended broken venetian blinds and patched oil cloth table coverings that were cigarette burned. Furniture thrown in the front yard was retrieved while it was still dark. (The neighbors must not know what had taken place earlier that night.)

Because of Paw Paw's government check, money should not have been a problem. Alcoholism caused their dilemma. After a few days spent in bars Paw Paw came home "drunk and broke."

Lies, discipline and sewing lessons

Nick learned honesty at an early age. He was fascinated watching Nanny "tat" flowers out of string. One day she remarked that she could make better flowers if she had a tatting shuttle. (This is a lost art.) Since tatting shuttles cost a nickel, she couldn't afford to buy one.

The next time they were at Kress' 5 $ 10 he pocketed one. Later at home he got out the shuttle and asked her to tat him a flower. She inquired where he had gotten the shuttle. He lied, "I bought it at Kress'." "You stole this" she accused, knowing he didn't have any money. She didn't finish the flower and nothing further was said.

Two or three months later they were at Kress' again. Nanny asked to see the store manager. "My son stole this from your store," she announced and handed him the shuttle. Nick thought to himself, "I'm going to the penitentiary!" and was scared to death. The manager, understanding the point Nan was trying to make, told Nick that if he ever stole from the store again he would go to jail! Nick left totally chastened.

Honesty, discipline and doing things the "right way" were learned early. An example: when he began hanging clothes on the clothesline he hung up whatever he found first. Wash cloths were hung next to sheets which were hung next to towels. He quickly learned this was not the way things were done in the Nicholson back yard. He had to rehang the entire wash (wash cloths all together, sheets all together, etc.)

Money and food was obviously scarce, but In spite of this Nanny's compassionate nature could never turn away those in need. Many times Nick observed her handing out sandwiches to those who came to the back door hungry.

Promptness was a high priority at least for Nanny. In spite of being reminded time after time to "come home at 4:00pm," whenever Nick became engrossed in a game the message was forgotten. "Here comes your mom, Moe!" someone would shout. Nick would cut out down the opposite side of the street hoping to reach the safety of home before Nanny could catch him. He needn't have bothered certain punishment awaited him anyway.

Amazingly, Nanny took time to play ball with Nick and his friends. He recalls she could throw pretty hard.

Life in Dayton

Nick was born in Dayton, Texas, and the family lived there five years before relocating in Houston. Who knows how Nanny learned to shoot earlier in life—but she was a crack shot. Maybe when ammunition is expensive and a "meal" for your family is on the line, you learn quickly. Norman, still very young admiringly told his father when he came home, "damn, Daddy, Momma killed two rabbits with one shot today!" She killed the rabbits because they were eating vegetables she had planted. Other times squirrels and rabbits were shot for food.

In later years after Paw Paw developed serious health issues he wanted to return to live in the country. Who knows why. Perhaps he remembered those as the happiest times of his life. Nan however had different memories of the country. "Me and my kids almost starved to death in the country. I'm not going back!" She also considered J.J.'s fragile health and knew she couldn't deal with it by herself. She had never even learned to drive a car. J.J. had discovered the sober life too late.

Both Nick and I were born during the war years and have vague memories of WW 2. It was such a dramatic time in our history—that even as small children we were affected. Nick remembers being frightened of seeing an airplane overhead and running all the way home.

I have only one strong recollection of the war—actually two. The first one involved ration books. To my childish mind you would simply give a stamp to a store clerk and not have to pay any money! It seemed like a good thing. The other memory concerned "blackouts." These were enforced throughout the country. At designated times all house and store lights must be turned off after dark. This made sense in Houston, Tx., located on the ship channel. Obviously vital goods for the war effort were shipped from there. However blackouts in Iowa were totally senseless. No one could seriously believe that either Japanese or German planes would fly that far to bomb cornfields.

Nick remembers having several fears. After moving to Houston from the country he steadfastly refused to talk on that big black instrument (the telephone). He once innocently inserted a hairpin into an electric socket and received a serious shock. He found daily life in the city frightening.

Ours was a world of ice-boxes, attic and/or window fans, wringer washing machines—or worse, scrub boards. We had 45 RPM records, radio was fairly new and there were no TVs. Some complaints heard circulating, "when cigarettes get to 35 cents a package I'm going to quit! "or "can you believe gas is now 50 cents a gallon?" A popular song of that era was "milkman keep those bottles quiet!" (The person who wrote the song worked shift work.) Milk and ice were both delivered to the house.

Nick enjoyed watching his mother patch clothes also a lost art. She took precise stitches always the same length and distance apart. One morning in boot camp several years later, the recruits were required to stamp their names on labels then sew them on their socks. They were to be sewn 1" from the top in the middle.

During inspection of their gear called junk on the bunk the drill instructor stopped and looked at Nick's socks. "Who sewed these?" he demanded. "Private Nicholson sewed them." "You're lying!" "No, sir, Private Nicholson sewed them." He yelled to the assistant drill instructor. "Get the whole platoon over here. I want everyone to sew on their patches like this—or I will refuse them!" He turned back to Nick. "Where did you learn to sew like that?" "Private Nicholson learned from his mother, Sir."

It was probably a good thing that a popularity contest was not held that day—guess who would have come in dead last!

Life with siblings

Nick's oldest brother, Sidney Joined the Marines four days after Pearl Harbor at the age of seventeen. Sidney's influence was probably one of the reasons Nick would later join the Corps. Sid's entire outfit was wiped out. He had developed Malaria prior to "shipping over" and that is probably the only reason he is alive today. Following the war he got a job on the "extra board" with the Southern Pacific Railroad. This means they call if they need extra help. From there he eventually rose to the responsible position of Trainmaster with the railroad.

For several years, he helped the family financially. Buying Nick's school clothes was one way.

His next older brother Dan is deceased. Nick and Dan were probably most alike in looks and personality. Their interests however were very different. Dan loved animals. He would rise early in the morning to feed his horses before going to work. He married his teenage sweetheart, Margie. They were happily married until his unexpected death in 2009. Livestock was a lifelong interest for Dan.

Years ago Nick's sister and I took a ceramic class together. Dan somehow got involved and surprised us all with his artistic ability. He painted an ashtray with a branding iron logo on it. He completed other projects that showed real talent (all with western emblems!) He and Margie lived on several acres of land in Highlands, Texas, They owned several hundred head of cattle as well as a feed store.

Who exactly is whom?

We had always known Nick and Dan looked somewhat alike, but what a surprise! Nick and I had a fun foto taken while on vacation several years ago. When we saw the picture my first reaction was, "Dan Nicholson!" We were posed in western wear something neither Nick nor I ever wore. I was decked out in a short skirt, fishnet hose and toting a six gun. Nick wore a ten gallon hat and looked for all the world like Dan's double.

When we showed the picture to Dan he asked to borrow it to play a joke on some friends. When he showed them the picture of him and "this ole gal" (they didn't know me) the joke was on him. He couldn't convince them that it was "really my younger brother and his wife!" They were appalled that he would be unfaithful to Margie! He probably had to call on her to establish his innocence! (Nick and I are pictured on the next page.)

NICK AND I IN WESTERN GEAR

Norman, who also went by "Nick" is the youngest brother. He was also the most colorful character in the family during his growing up years. He was attracted to the wild habits of Paw Paw and probably had the closest relationship with him of any of his sons. Norman acquired a reputation for playing hooky and hiding out to read "funny books." In the eighth grade he hit a principal and knocked him down a flight of stairs. The principal's mistake was trying to remove Norman's cigarettes from his shirt pocket. That ended the necessity of attending school—any school.

Norman the great equalizer

Norman and Nick were not especially close, but one incident stands out in Nick's memory. He and his buddy Charles Turnage played basketball regularly at Denver Harbor Park. They were thirteen at the time and seventeen year olds were using the court. When approached, they sarcastically objected to sharing the court with "kids." Backed by the fact that he and Charles played basketball from daylight to dark every day they could and the brash bravado of thirteen year olds, they issued a challenge. They declared they would spot the older teens 20 points and beat them in a 21 point game.

Unable to resist such a ridiculous bet they agreed. True to their word, Nick and Charles shellacked them 21-20. This was too much for the 17 year old ring leader to bear. He decked Nick with one punch. "Wait here," Nick commanded as he picked himself up off the ground.

He and Charles rode their bikes to Norman's house and told their story. Norman would have fought anyone just for the sheer pleasure, but to have a righteous cause as well was too good to resist. Sure enough the teens were waiting. As they were soon to discover this was not wise decision. Norman a seasoned street fighter administered a decisive beating, got back in his car and returned home. After word got around, Nick and Charles weren't bothered again.

Family members in crises

Years later, Norman was hunting on his property near Conroe, Texas. By this time he and his wife Ruby owned a store and a large farm. He had done well in spite of a rocky start. Norman was hunting alone at night with his weapon strapped to his back. A limb broke under his weight and he fell to the ground. The weapon broke his spine in two places.

He lay there for quite some time and fired shot after shot to signal his wife, but no one came. Finally in desperation he fired his last shot. Thankfully that time Ruby and the others who were searching, heard the sound and rescued him. Ants had severely bitten his ears and face, but he did not go into shock.

Life Flight couldn't be used to take him to the hospital. It was so wooded there was no place to land. Darkness may also have been a factor. Instead he had to make the long trip to Houston by ambulance. At one point we were afraid we would lose him. Following his recovery, in spite of all the facts to the contrary, he vowed he would one day walk again. Anyone who knew Norman believed if anyone could it would be him.

He worked with "Dr Ed" for years because Ed assured him he could make him walk. Many dollars and years of pain and effort later, even Norman realized it wouldn't happen. Norman was to remain a paraplegic.

Nick and I have often wondered how we would have measured up in Norman's situation. Through all those years he and Ruby, his wife and devoted companion, showed us all what courage and perseverance looked like up close.

Nick's sister Ann, (not her full name) was destined to inherit a nickname she probably enjoyed even less than her given name, if that's possible. However she loves her family and endures "Pee Wee" with as much grace as she can muster. Even before but especially since Nan died Ann is the glue that keeps the family together. A widow, she's the one who goes to see Norman up on his farm (much farther north than Conroe.) She also checks on Sidney, who lives in Lufkin and is in fragile health. She remembers the birthdays of all family members and finds time and energy to socialize with both family and friends. Did I mention she usually works a 40 hour work week?

Ann had a very long and difficult illness many years ago. She had to spend a year being treated in Denver, Colorado, all the while coping with marriage issues. She and Norman are our heroes. They both endured personal tragedies and came through triumphantly!

Along with Norman and Ann, Nick had a demon of his own to confront. It was fear. Fear of his father, but an even greater fear that when he left home (to join the Marines) that his mother would not be safe. There would be no one to protect her from his father's drunken rages. The other kids were now married and had homes and families of their own.

It became necessary as stated before to find a job while still in high school. He went to work in a downtown department store called Rolle-Jewett and Beck. His boss was Mr. Harvey Barber. He became not only a father figure to Nick, but also a role model and mentor. Mr. Barber was a former Marine. He had visions of grooming Nick as his successor at the company.

Although Nick had discovered a love for selling he knew retail sales were not for him. They entailed long hours, work on weekends with not enough compensation. He started out stocking and marking merchandise and four years later was the buyer and assistant manager of the department. He ended his retail career to enlist.

Mr. Barber was both happy and sad. Sad to see him leave, but happy he had made the decision to become a Marine.

Nick learned some valuable lessons in those four years. The most important one he learned from Jim Fandall, the assistant manager. Nick took his place when Mr. Fandall resigned a short time later.

Nick firmly believed he should be making more money per hour. There were no automatic cost of living raises back then. He approached Mr. Fandall and asked him to speak to Mr. Barber regarding a raise for him. Nick was afraid to ask. Jim advised him, "in this world, you're going to have to learn to toot your own horn. No one will do it for you! Besides, you are doing a good job. He'll probably give it to you—but you have to ask!" Nick did ask—and Mr. Barber did grant the raise. Valuable lesson learned.

As mentioned earlier, Nick had a "fear" to overcome. If confronting your worst fear is a sign of maturity, Nick took a definite step toward maturity late one night after work. After arriving home late, as he did each Thursday night, he "had it out" with his father. As far back as anyone could remember the whole family had lived in mortal fear. Namely, that one night in a drunken stupor he would kill them all. He had a .45 caliber pistol that he kept at home.

On the bus, as Nick made his way home after work, he vowed to take action if his dad called his mother one more foul word. He said his stomach was in knots. His real fear was that once he began, he would vent on Paw Paw all the pent-up rage he had held inside for years. Soon after his arrival at home, his dad, drunk and foul mouthed, uttered a curse directed at Nanny. Without warning, Nick knocked him over the kitchen table shattering the venetian blinds behind him. He followed with a few more blows, yelling all the while, "if you ever curse or lay a hand on her again, I'll kill you!"

After that his anger spent, Nick took him to the bathroom and washed the blood off and doctored his cuts and bruises. Usually when you stand up to a bully and call his bluff, it ends the abuse. That's what happened in this case.

Years later, when I entered the family, I already knew of Paw Paw's legendary escapades. By that time he was old and broken in health. He said to me one day, "I pray God will forgive me of my many sins!" I "saw his soul" that day and prayed with him. Until the day she died, I never heard Nanny say a harsh or condemning word about him. I suspect it was for the same reason I felt compassion toward him; he allowed her to see his soul. She had seen him at his worst and at his best. I'm not sure if I had been the object of his abuse as she was, that I could have handled it with her mercy and grace.

Nick, at this point, has now closed the door on his adolescence. He is about to open the door to an adventure that will leave its mark on him for the rest of his life. First, let's talk about . . . .

Life with the next generation

Sonny, Sid Jr., spent a lot of time at Nanny and Paw Paw's house while Nick was growing up. Sid and his first wife Betty both worked. Sonny was like the younger brother Nick never had. He would take him along when he played basketball or had baseball practice at Denver Harbor Athletic Field. Sonny would obediently sit for hours watching whatever game was being played. When he attended a game that Nick was pitching, he would loudly yell, "strike him out, Un' Moe!"

One morning when Sonny was about 2 years old, Sid was bringing him to Nanny's for the day. Aggravated by the way his car was stalling as he turned a corner, Sid uttered an expletive. Sonny was listening in the back seat. The next day and for weeks afterwards whenever Sid drove around that corner Sonny would repeat the expletive.

Blessed with an intelligent and inquisitive mind, Sonny read encyclopedias as recreational reading. He enjoyed the academic life and settled on dentistry as his life work. He especially loved the out-of-doors, a love shared by his son, Scott. Years later, Nick, brother Sid, Sonny and Scott, now grown up, indulged their love of fishing in Canada and later Alaska.

Although the rest of us (Linda, later Scott's wife, Paula and I) would have loved to be fishing in Canada or Alaska, as the case might be—we made the best of it! In spite of our dearest wish to be out there in the wilds in a smelly fishing camp we didn't once complain! We whiled away the lonely hours by shopping, travel, friends, etc. Just doing whatever we could to pass the time.

Linda usually with a daughter in tow, would head for the bright lights of New York. Linda has two attractions in New York now. Laurie, daughter number one has a little one named Coralie Suzette. Kristy, daughter number two works as a beautician in Tulsa. She has a teaching degree but loves her work as a beautician more. Paula, meanwhile is busy working and caring for Abraham, Levi and Isaac. Sid's daughter, Pat, is married to Frank Bailey a lawyer in Mountain Home, Arkansas. She has a career at the University of Arkansas holding the position of Provost.

The fishing group began their trips in the calm serenity of Canada before tackling the wilds of Alaska. They met and quickly became friends with John Jacobs. John is a professional fishing guide there in Canada. He loves Canadian winters. If the temperature reaches 80 degrees he claims that he is "cooking" meaning unbearably hot.

He told about the time his son—also adverse to warm weather—was waiting for the school bus one morning. The temperature was 45 degrees below zero. The boy decided to wait inside the house explaining that it was "a mite chilly this morning." John tried to persuade the group to come up to do some ice fishing, but had no takers.

One day when John, Nick and Sid were out in a boat fishing the alarm on sid's watch kept going off. Sid was hard of hearing and wasn't aware of the sound. After the alarm went off three or four times it became irritating to both John and Nick. John asked to see Sid's watch. When he questioned why, John declared he intended to throw it in the lake! Nick and John laughed, but Sid didn't find it amusing

Alaska, land of bears and salmon

NICK SHOWING OFF HIS CATCH.
SONNY IS CLEANING FISH IN THE BACKGROUND.

The group later went to Alaska salmon fishing for several years in a row. Grizzly bears occasionally showed up to compete for the Salmon. One day Sonny and Scott returned from fishing with nothing to show for their efforts. They were teased for being inept fishermen. They said with all sincerity a bear had eaten their fish. "A likely story," was the response.

The very next day Nick and Sid encountered the same situation. As they were wading in knee-high to waist-deep water Nick saw movement. There on top of a hill was a grizzly headed toward them. Nick started backing out of the water. "Let's go!" he yelled to Sid. "Why?" Sid shouted back. Nick pointed in the direction of the bear. Sid took a bucket out of a boat anchored at the dock. He started swinging it trying in vain to drive the animal away. He knew the bear's goal was to eat their fish tied on a stringer in the water nearby. As they watched the huge, hungry grizzly swimming rapidly toward them, they quickly decided to relinquish their catch. When they got a safe distance away they watched the bear greedily eat every fish on the stringer.

One day after fishing Scott discovered his billfold was missing from the top pocket of his waders. This of course presented a serious problem. Without a driver's license Scott would be unable to board the flight home. They went to the airport, the hub of activity in Yakatat. A flight was scheduled at 4:00pm and another at 9:00am. Between these times the airport was closed. It was late afternoon and the airport was open. They could check to see if the billfold had been turned in. It hadn't. Ordinarily the next best thing would have been to have Scott's birth certificate fedexed from Oklahoma but they knew his mom was in New York. No one was home and Scott was still unmarried at this time.

To their surprise and delight the billfold had been recovered! Upon returning to the fishing camp they learned the welcome news. The person who found it didn't even leave his name! That day they found out just how tightly bonded fishermen really are! (Bonding aside, Nick pointed out that truth occasionally flies out the window when describing the size of the catch.)

STEERS, BRONCOS AND BROKEN FENCE BOARDS

Dan Nicholson, Sr. loved all things Western. Just as Sid's love of hunting and fishing influenced both son and grandson—Dan's boys were likewise influenced. Both Danny and Steve enjoyed the rodeo atmosphere. Dan constructed a pen where the boys could practice calf roping, bulldogging and bronc riding. They invited their friends to participate and to bring their girlfriends to watch the spectacle on the weekends.

One fateful Sunday afternoon Danny was bulldogging a steer. The steer hugged the fence and Danny's leg was caught between the animal and a broken fence board. The board pierced his thigh causing serious injury.

At the hospital the wound was cleaned. Danny received a hundred and fifty five stitches inside his thigh, and ten on the outside of the wound. He also retained some splinters inadvertently overlooked. For several months and years after, these splinters festered and had to be removed. (Thank you, Lord that he can still walk.)

Steve also was a bull rider but unlike brother Danny escaped serious injury. Danny, a welder, who has worked for National Oil Well Corp for years is a dedicated Astro fan! Steve works as a procurement officer. His company has been sold to other, larger companies once or twice. Fortunately he has retained and prospered at his job. He is also a golfer. Both guys have obviously had to retire from bronc riding and calf roping!

CHAPTER 3

THE MEANEST DRILL INSTRUCTOR IN THE WORLD!

Every Marine who goes through boot camp is firmly convinced that he had the meanest possible drill instructor. Nick is no exception.

Nick left home for the very first time when he joined the Corps. It was his first airplane trip and first time out of Texas. He had two buddies who said they would enlist with him but didn't show.

We calculated the time and date that Nick left for camp. I would have been scheduled to work at Braniff's ticket counter that day. He could have passed me on the way to board his flight, but we were not to meet for a couple of years.

Upon their arrival the drill instructor in charge "welcomes" the new recruits en masse. His message can be summed up in this statement, "you guys are the worst bunch of recruits I've ever seen! There is no way we can make Marines out of you—but we will try!" Warmed by this encouraging greeting the recruits are issued clothing, have their heads shaved then led to their barracks. Nick was about to enter the worst—and ultimately one of the best—experiences of his life.

He soon met his senior D.I. It was memorable. Nick describes him as the strongest man he had ever seen. He demonstrated this by doing fifty one arm pushups in front of the astonished group. He also proved he was the meanest and most foul-mouthed as well. Solty did, however, have the attention and respect of the new arrivals.

His name and personality became indelibly imprinted in Nick's mind: Staff Sergeant Charles Soltysiak.

CHARLES SOLTYSIAK
"Obviously the toughest D. I. in the Marine Corps."

About an hour after he introduced himself Soltysiak grabbed one startled recruit by the collar, "what's my name, private?" he demanded. "Sir, Sergeant Salty jack, sir." The punishment that followed probably made the poor boot wish he had never even <u>heard</u> of the Corps. Soltysiak constantly warned all within the sound of his voice, "I will beat you severely about the head and shoulders!"

The underlying principle of the Marine Corps, to the uninitiated, is to convince each man that he is "lower than whale dung that lies at the bottom of the ocean." Day after day the unit is trained to arrive at one single thought, "I hate this place and I loathe and detest my drill instructor!"

To accomplish this, each small infraction or miscue is punished harshly. Hours will be spent running and carrying weapons while wearing combat boots. Nick reports that at times he was so tired he literally couldn't see. Everything was black. For the first time in his life he learned what it meant to "get your second wind." To add to their misery, showers were taken in cold water in a tin building open at both ends to the cold San Diego night air.

The Marine Corps is at war with the civilian world. All contact with the outside world is eliminated. No radios, TVs, telephones or personal items are allowed. It's impossible for the rest of us who were never in this environment, to realize how completely regimented it is. Not even the tiniest detail is overlooked. With monotonous regularity each man is reminded that he had enlisted in the D.I.'s beloved Corps and must never bring reproach on its name.

For Nick there was an extra price to pay. He lost his precious hair. In civilian life, he wore it Elvis style in a high pompadour with a ducktail in the back. The tight fitting band inside the steel helmet cut off circulation. When he consulted a doctor on the base he was given that information. He recalls with horror waking to find mounds of hair left on his pillow.

I have never known Nick when he had hair. I've only seen pictures. They were enough for me to sincerely assure him that he looks better without hair. The old saying, "bald is beautiful" is true of him. Of course, given a choice, I'm sure he would opt for hair.

Reveille sounded at 4:00am. Those failing to get up quickly were assisted by having their bunks turned over on top of them. This traumatic experience became deeply ingrained. Even after we were married when the alarm went off, Nick began to thrash wildly about. I would begin speaking soothingly to him before I was fully awake. "Nick, it's okay, you're no longer in the corps!"

If I thought about the Marine Corps at all, I would have imagined the men relaxing at lunch time with loud laughter and light-hearted camaraderie Nick found this amusing and far from reality. There was no conversation, light-hearted or otherwise. The only sound was the voice of the D.I. counting. "Counting what?" you might ask. On the count of "one" every member of Nick's platoon eating in the mess hall, raised a fork with food from his plate. On the count of "two" the food was taken into each mouth, on the count of "three" the fork was withdrawn and suspended in air awaiting the final count. At the count of "four" forks were again lowered to the plate to begin the process again.

The official name for overweight recruits was "fat a—es." They were compelled to wait at the back of the line until everyone else was served. The D.I. accompanied them through the line ordering "no potatoes, no bread, no desserts!" Penalties for smuggling food were severe!

About midway through basic training Nick came down with the measles. He knew he would have to start boot camp over again if the measles were discovered. He stuck it out undetected, firing on the rifle range even though very sick.

For the most part Nick stayed out of trouble. He did get punched in the gut for some infraction and lost a front tooth for saying "I" instead of "Pvt. Nicholson." Pity the poor enlistee who had a habit of bouncing when he marched. Punishment was swift and severe. Some had no sense of rhythm and had a hard time learning to march in step. Worse case scenario: falling down on "the grinder" while running with your platoon. If this happened the man was simply run over.

One of Nick's friends made a grave error. To Sgt. Soltysiak it was an opportunity to irritate a recruit—an opportunity never to be missed. Manuel made the mistake of throwing a rock at a pigeon for whatever reason. It turned out according to Solty that Manuel was trying to kill his favorite pigeon in all the world. For the remaining time in boot camp Manuel had to "keep the area free of pigeons." Every time the Sarg spotted one Manuel would be called upon. He had to drop whatever he was doing and chase away the offending bird.

Yes, it's brain-washing. Once the recruits whether law students or street people began to think alike the real training started. The secret to the Marine Corps is that all the parts are interchangeable. Each man is taught to lead. If the ranking officer is incapacitated the next man is equipped to take over. The squad, battalion, whatever, goes on without missing a beat.

A couple of years ago Nick, some friends and I went to San Diego. We were privileged to see a group graduate to become full-fledged marines. Drill instructors took part in the ceremony. I remember one in particular. As he strode across the field with ramrod posture swagger stick in hand everything about him proclaimed, "I'm the best!" and he was reveling in the moment. It was easy to understand the lure of the dress blues.

The joy of completing boot camp!

After the completion of boot training came combat training. It's hard for us civilians to understand what a privilege it is to be able to unbutton the top button on your dungaree shirt. It means everything to a new Marine. It tells those in command you have completed boot camp and you deserve, and are entitled to, respect! This begins the healing process for those who have endured the humiliation of basic training. In the way that boot camp molded the mind of the marine, now combat training would build the morale and the physique.

BOOT CAMP IS OVER! NOTE THE UNBUTTONED SHIRT.

Before progressing to combat training at Camp Pendleton two weeks of mess duty were required. It was dreaded because it was dull, hard physical work. All utensils, dishes, tables and floors must be scrubbed and/or mopped after each meal. By the time one round of cooking and cleaning was completed it was time to begin the process all over again.

Mess duty proved to be a blessing in disguise for Nick. He and some friends had gotten their first liberty since enlistment. They headed to Long Beach. Nick and who knows how many others, celebrated a little too much. Nick fell asleep on the beach in the sun and this resulted in the worst sunburn of his life. It was an excruciating experience to dress in uniform and return to camp. Reporting for duty in this condition is a court martial offense. Mess duty was a blessing because two compassionate cooks hid him for four days until he was able to dress again.

Fond memories of the obstacle course

Before completing combat training each man must experience the obstacle course. The simple objective of this training is to survive. Probably no one would list this as his favorite training activity. A machine gun mounted in concrete fires live ammo 36" above the ground. To successfully navigate the course it's obviously necessary to get up close and personal with mother earth.

Each guy must crawl along the ground using mainly his elbows and knees to move him forward. Of course the necessary rifle is always in hand. This weapon, barrel pointed up, won't fire if it's contaminated with dirt.

These conditions are simply not entertaining enough for the powers that be. To insure their undivided attention, 4' X 4' squares of explosives ((TNT) are surrounded by sandbags and placed throughout the course. They are blown up randomly and the concussion can bounce a man off the ground. Objective: get back down as quickly as you can. This could happen more than once. These explosives are set off by a Marine working in a tower overlooking the course.

Everyone's favorite: crawling down into a hole crossing it and climbing back out. Everyone knew it was necessary to come out of the hole "sideways" because of the ever-present bullets overhead. Fortunately this technique was demonstrated beforehand.

Also scoring high in popularity: culverts. The trainees are required to crawl approximately 50' in darkness covered in silt that gets in the nose and mouth. Holding the rifle aloft in these conditions can be challenging. After all that, sitting in a hole as a 48 ton tank rolls over you has to be a piece of cake! When asked how long all this takes, the answer is forever. Actual time: 30-40 minutes.

At the end of combat training each man emerges convinced he is invincible, ready for battle and eager for an opportunity to prove it. One such situation almost presented itself during Nick's time in service. Nick's tank battalion unit was scheduled to leave for Lebanon during a Middle-East crisis. At the last minute it was cancelled. Dreams of glory and earning a congressional medal of honor were dashed. (I, for one, say "thank You, Lord!")

About two months ago Nick decided to check the internet to see if he could find any information about his old D.I. Staff Sergeant Soltysiak. Assisted by our son Mark he located his name. "Solty" had passed away just the month before.

Nick talked to his widow, Olga. "Oh did you know my beloved Charley?" she asked. Nick nearly dropped the phone in shock. He could never have conceived of Charles Soltsiak described in those terms! His old Sarge had died with Alzheimer's disease. He must have mellowed in his later years to be remembered with such fondness. Nick sent her pictures of himself in the Corps and of our family and she expressed her gratitude.

"Some people spend an entire lifetime wondering if they made a difference in this world. Marines don't have that problem."

President Ronald Reagan

Trouble in the Tank Battalion

Private first class Lebate, for reasons known only to him, walked in and out of the barracks several times. Each time he left he would slam the door so hard it opened again. The barracks was never warm enough by design so having the door constantly left open was an added irritation. Pfc. Chandler who had a bunk close to the offending door closed it each time.

When Lebate entered again Chandler remarked to him that he was wearing out the door! As Lebate prepared to leave once more, Chandler asked him to close the door properly so it would lock. It didn't happen.

This time when Lebate returned Chandler stood to confront him. Without warning Lebate reached into his pack, drew out his bayonet and plunged it into Chandler's arm.

This took place after all training had been completed. Nick by this time was a corporal and in charge of the barracks. When Chandler yelled in pain Nick knew it was his job to take over. He confronted Lebate, still standing there with bayonet in hand. "You put that down, lay it down, Lebate!" Fortunately he did.

Nick applied a tourniquet improvised by using someone's belt. He stuck as much of his hand as would fit into the wound. With each heartbeat blood squirted everywhere. Nick was later to say "it felt like hot catsup!" He ordered someone to go notify the officer of the day and report that a man had been stabbed; that medics and an ambulance were needed right away. Chandler by this time had lost a lot of blood. He was in danger of passing out or going into shock.

A large crowd had now gathered. To everyone's intense relief corpsmen and a stretcher arrived soon afterwards. Chandler spent several days in the hospital but no one ever saw Lebate again. His fate was kept a closely guarded secret. Nick surmised that he was probably court martialed.

Nick was given a meritorious mass. Civilians not acquainted with the Corps would say, "was that all?" To a Marine it's like getting to meet God. When the officer of the day reported the incident to the Battalion Commander, Colonel Jeter invited him to his office for a brief conversation. He congratulated him on saving a Marine's life and shook his hand. After that Nick returned to his duties and life in the barracks returned to normal.

After the Corps—now what?

NICK IN CIVVIES LEAVING THE CORPS

Nick was definitely at loose ends after the Corps. He considered re-enlisting. He was told before he was discharged, that the nation was in a recession and It would be difficult to find a civilian job. He thought that was Marine propaganda but unfortunately, found it to be true.

Among his options were possible jobs at Shell Oil Co. and Champion Paper but These companies did not have openings yet. He awaited the first vacancy. (We had not met at this time. This will be related a few paragraphs down.) After we had dated for some time he read me a letter from Captain Stein of the USMC.

The first paragraph stated "Morris E Nicholson, just recently released from active duty in the United States Marine Corps in the rank of sergeant, was a member of my section for a period of approximately eighteen months during which time he always displayed all the qualities of a good Marine. Not the least of these were maturity of mind not found in most young men of his age." The letter concluded that he had Captain Stein's unqualified recommendation as to character and would be a valuable asset in any business operation. I knew almost nothing about the Marine Corps but realized the significance of such a letter. I told him years later the letter was one of the main reasons I married him! In truth there were many others as well. Nick has never been and probably never will be a patient person. At this time in his life he was forced to sit and contemplate his future. His priorities were: To work at a selling job. Find someone to marry and settle down. Have a larger, nicer house than his parents had. Start a family. If you had asked him he would not have listed these, but down deep these were his goals.

If he re-enlisted as he was tempted to do, his superior officers wanted him to go to OCS. This was attractive but at this point in his life the Marine Corps would probably never have enabled him to reach his other goals. To help pass the time and bring in some money he got a job in a convenience store. His brother-in-law Wayne recommended him to the store owner Leonard Ivy.

We meet—in a grocery store!

This store was a block from the garage apartment I shared with Bernice Guidry who also worked at Braniff Airways. Nick and I had a few short, casual conversations but one day I gave him a check. I was going to the beach the next day with Bernice and we needed some cash. When I saw Bernice that afternoon I casually mentioned there was a "cute guy" at the store, that she ought to check him out. She did, but when she returned she announced, "he's not cute at all!" (Nick went on break and she was definitely right about the other guy!)

After our weekend at the beach I went back to the store a few days later. Nick shocked me by saying, "is your name Beverly Lunn?" "Yes." He replied accusingly "you gave me a hot check!" Actually it wasn't. It was his way of getting my attention—and he did, because there was a real possibility that it was hot! Following "coke" dates in the afternoons he began calling me for evening dates. He had copied my phone number off my check. Nick certainly got a lot of mileage out of that check!

A few months later I was invited to Thanksgiving dinner at his house. Wild man Norman was cautioned against using bad language and everyone was warned to be on their best behavior. I for my part, was also trying to make a good impression so we were all pretty uptight during that meal.

At last Champion Paper came through for Nick and he went to work in Pasadena, Texas. Some people called it "Stinkadina" because of the foul smell associated with manufacturing paper. Nick's work car was an old beat-up Chevrolet. Employees' cars in the lot were showered daily with an acid-rain like substance that literally ate away the exterior of the car.

He started out sweeping floors and worked up to "trimmer helper." Nick was temperamentally and physically unsuited for shift work. It was an ordeal. His parents' house on Woolworth was not air-conditioned and during Houston's hot summer days, it was next to impossible to sleep. Later when we married, Bernice moved out and Nick moved into our garage apartment. Here at least there was a window unit. This luxury was offset by our landlord, Mr. Johnson's untimely use of his chainsaw just as Nick got to sleep.

Nick and Roy Shelton worked as a team cutting paper—large amounts of it at a time. A huge, extremely sharp knife came down with great force to trim off the excess paper. It was Nick's job to position the paper then get his hands out of the way quickly, as Roy operated the knife. Nick trusted Roy but I didn't. Roy was accident prone! ("Sorry" seems rather inadequate if you have sliced off someone's hands!) All in all this was not a job made in heaven.

A wedding scheduled for Friday the 13th

We set our wedding for June 13 of the following year. It turned out to be Friday the 13th. Since our marriage has lasted fifty two plus years apparently it was a good day. My parents, brother Dick and sister Sandy came down for the wedding. By today's standards it was frugal since neither of our families were affluent. The trip down and back from Iowa probably cost a lot more than the wedding.

Our families bonded and it was agreed that distance really made no difference. We could easily have lived next door to each other. Nick especially enjoyed meeting my father Johnny and he loved Nick in return. God was good in providing several men to fill this void. When Dad died years later it was hard for both of us to bear.

At dad's funeral during an Iowa winter, the ground was frozen solid and so were we. Neither Nick nor I had a heavy coat to wear during the graveside service. Nick especially suffered that day!

We had to leave Grinnell early the next morning to catch the flight home. Brother Dick, by then about eighteen, planned to go with us to bring the car back from Des Moines. The Volkswagen behind us in the driveway had at least an inch of ice and the door wouldn't open, so the guys had to physically move it out of the way.

The snow was coming down in sheets as we made our way cautiously to Des Moines. Nick had no experience in driving on snow-packed highways. A couple of miles out of Grinnell Dick said diplomatically, "I'm afraid you're going to miss your flight unless we drive faster." Nick gladly surrendered the wheel. With Dick driving, our speed picked up significantly.

We were the last to board the flight; they closed the door right behind us. There wasn't even time to tell Dick "thanks and goodbye!" The total cost of the trip was $6.00. Obviously Braniff didn't consider us high priority passengers so wouldn't have worried about leaving us behind.

Nick had to get back home to work his shift. When he got out of bed to go to Champion, he found he couldn't turn his head! He had to call in sick and go to the chiropractor instead. So much for Iowa in the winter.

All four of our parents are now deceased. Nick and I do keep in touch with my brother and sister and their spouses as much as we can. For many years I traveled back and forth to see Sandy and Bob who still live in Grinnell, Iowa, the town where I grew up. For years now Sandy and I have had a running debate about who has come to see whom the most. Let me settle it once and for all—I have done the most traveling! Sandy, you'll have to write your own book and make your own claim!

We don't get to see their sons, Chris and Kurt very often, but they are sweethearts and we enjoy them when we can. Kurt and Melissa married just this past year.

Chris is built like a lumberjack and enjoys construction work. He has his own house in Grinnell and lives there with his latest dog. The last one I knew was named Bruno, but there probably have been others since. Chris actually should live in Canada. He's an outdoorsman who would enjoy living off the land! As rugged as Chris looks on the outside to those of us who know and love him, he's a teddy bear!

For several years Nick and I lost contact with Dick and Carol. They have now settled in McKinney, Texas close to Mark and Julie. Since then we've spent a lot of fun hours with them, their two sons, Josh and Jeremy and their wives. We need to find out Dick and Carol's secret. Both sons and their families live in McKinney. Josh and Renae might break ranks and move, but Jeremy and Cindy are firmly entrenched there with their two girls, Bella and Vicki. Josh and Ranae have three, Caleb, Chloe and Keira. It is an unwritten rule in the Lunn family: all children must have red hair. Only Caleb has dared to be blonde!

Terror in Breckenridge Park!

Following our wedding we honeymooned in San Antonio. As we strolled one day in Breckenridge Park there to Nick's consternation, was a large pack of dogs also strolling in the park. I've always loved dogs and had no fear of them whatsoever. Nick had gone to great lengths to impress me with his strength and bravery as a Marine. This bravery however did not extend to dogs. He had grown up petrified of dogs especially big ones traveling in large numbers. I called one or two of them over to pat them and make friends. Nick turned ashen. It wasn't until years later I learned of his deep-seated fear of these animals. In fact Nick has a distrust of most four legged creatures. He would not be considered an animal lover in any sense of the word.

Back to reality . . . .

After the honeymoon we returned to life in our garage apartment. It was "L" shaped surrounding a bedroom and bath. The only furnishings that could qualify as "adequate" were two sets of ceiling to floor draperies. When we moved into our first house these draperies would be cut in half and used to cover four windows much shorter in length.

Our real pride and joy (not!) was our TV. It had rabbit ears on top wrapped in aluminum foil, which was supposed to help reception. It was housed in a metal casing supported by metal legs. We changed channels by using a fork from the kitchen. Actually, it looked pretty much at home with the rest of our furnishings. The apartment rented for $42.50 a month.

Before I met Nick, I went with a guy who liked prune whip. I had never heard of prune whip and had no idea how it was made. I bought a cookbook and found a recipe for it. When I completed the recipe it didn't taste like I had hoped it would. I kept adding more ingredients until it began to taste somewhat good so I pronounced it "finished!" The person I hoped to impress tasted it and thoughtfully reported it, "unlike any prune whip he had ever tasted."

I say all that to give you an idea of my cooking skills. The first meal I fixed for Nick after we were married was a frozen pot pie. Nanny was an excellent cook who fixed nearly everything from scratch. Also, his family had no money for a frozen anything. He was honestly baffled about what this item on his plate could possibly be! In time, Nanny in pity took me under her wing and taught me everything I know about cooking.

Our Mom was a career woman. She was a "registered" nurse a title of which she was extremely proud. Her nursing degree provided her sense of self-worth. Sandy followed in her footsteps. Unlike Mom, she never depended on nursing to fulfill her. Mom considered doctors "God." Sandy has a slightly different view that we won't discuss here. I admire Sandy's sense of fun and her laughter always just below the surface.

Mom never learned any skills while growing up at home, so she didn't especially enjoy house work—or cooking. Because of this she had no experience to pass on to us.

My brother, Dick, recently told me this story. When he and his wife were first married they went home to visit Mom and Dad. Both he and Carol smoked. Dick saw a dish on the counter that he assumed was garbage to be thrown out. He was looking for a convenient place to butt out his cigarette—so he butted it out in the dish of "garbage." He found out sometime later this was the dish Mom had planned to serve for dinner! It's unclear what happened after that. I don't know if he confessed and took everyone out to dinner, as he should have, or if he said nothing and ate from the opposite end of the dish!

Sister Sandy, unlike me, was destined to become an excellent cook. She too did not start out that way. For her first attempt at cooking a meal for Bob's relatives, she told me she cooked half of a chicken for each person. At least no one would walk away from that meal hungry.

Sandy and I were both graduates of the Verna Lunn Cooking School. Following graduation a post-graduate course in "Boiling Water Effectively" was offered.

Each of us has a year in life when we fully realize "we too will age!" Mine arrived earlier than most. I will never again be as old as I was at thirty. Sandy's fateful year came at fifty. It seems according to her, that she had teased her older friends so unmercifully, that when she "hit the wall" at fifty there was no sympathy forthcoming for her.

Down here in Houston I plotted a way to further rub it in. Grinnell is a small college town where everyone knows everyone else. I planned to contact the Smith Funeral Home there and arrange to have a hearse sent to deliver a fake funeral policy to her.

When I called her she already sounded so pitiful and depressed—not like her at all—I didn't have the heart to carry through.

Sandy's husband, Bob, was a gifted athlete who would beat me regularly in my tennis days when I came to Iowa. His real love was cross-country biking with a large group. These were well planned with mapped-out routes, support vehicles carrying food, water and first aid if necessary. Sandy sometimes went too when she was "coerced." They rode a bicycle built for two on these trips. Bob found he was doing a *lot* of peddling going up most hills.

SISTER-IN-LAW CAROL AND BROTHER DICK
LOOKING YOUNG AND BEAUTIFUL

SISTER SANDY AND BROTHER-IN-LAW BOB.
OH TO BE YOUNG AND GORGEOUS AGAIN.

CHAPTER 4

NICK, HOW DID YOU FIND ALL THOSE PEOPLE?

Knowing I was going to be writing this book, I jokingly asked Nick how he wanted to be remembered. I say "jokingly" because I already knew how he felt about questions of this nature. True to form he said, "that's the most ridiculous question I have ever heard. Actually, I like Tom Watson's quote: 'remember Tom Watson? He was a hellofa golfer!' I want to be remembered as someone who helped build a place to have fun and make a living."

Vendors who called on Apollo often asked Nick, "where did you get all these good people?" They were used to calling on companies with two or three outstanding employees, but were impressed with the overall quality of Apollo personnel.

Nick personally chose nearly every person who worked for the company. He sought them out. He would sometimes risk the ire of one of his customers by hiring one of their best workers. Especially in the early days as he made sales calls, he would also look for people he wanted to hire. (He made it a rule never to hire by resume.) He watched how the potential employee worked for their present company. They never had a clue they were being interviewed for a job. Often they hadn't even thought of making a career change until the offer was made. Nick preferred training employees from scratch. It was more time consuming but they didn't have preconceived ideas about "how things should be done."

My husband is one of those rare men who likes to communicate. When we were first married I loved to read. One of his first comments was, "put that book down and talk to me." He carried that same philosophy into business. He encouraged his employees to talk, not only to each other but also to him.

Nick's office door at work was seldom closed. When it was he had a sign on it that read "if you can get a new account or save an old one don't knock come on in." To insure communication the week began with a 7:30am sales meeting. He was fond of asking, "what time does the 7:30 sales meeting start?" Another "Nickism" was to say that if someone arrived at 7:30 he/she was late! Did I say he stressed punctuality?

Years ago a meeting was held that wives were expected to attend. I embarrassed my husband by being the only one to arrive late. My excuse was that I got lost on the way to the office. Somebody said, "well, at least it's obvious she doesn't often bother her husband at work." I was grateful someone saw something positive about it.

Each Wednesday at 7:30am a credit meeting was scheduled, and a bull session that afternoon after work.

There was no such thing as an eight hour day at Apollo. The day usually ended at 7:00pm or later. One employee observed that you had to put in a half a day at Apollo and Nick didn't care which twelve hours you worked.

Nick loved problems. "Companies don't like to switch suppliers if things are going well. However if you can find someone with a problem you can solve, save them money, or show them a better product they'll gladly change. Whatever the big paper companies won't do we will! We mainly sell service; we just happen to supply paper. People are looking for those who make their jobs easier."

He recalled one problem of which he was not particularly fond. An Apollo salesperson got a call from a very irate bank president regarding floor finish the bank recently applied to the lobby floor. He informed her that a customer had just slipped down "on Apollo's wax!" He demanded to speak to the owner. She warned Nick of the angry phone call he was about to receive.

As usual when faced with a potentially explosive situation, Nick was warm and affable. "Good morning, how can I help you?" The man introduced himself and said without further pleasantries, "about fifteen minutes ago, a customer fell down on your wax!" Nick had thought it through by this time. He interrupted politely, "Sir, I think what actually happened was your customer slipped down on <u>your</u> floor. It's quite possible there was a wet spot on <u>your</u> floor. If I were you I would contact your insurance company and deal with them." That was the last he heard of the incident.

Apollo trucks were always loaded to capacity and in a hurry. Westheimer Road a main Houston thoroughfare, was noted for its deep pot holes. One day after a particularly heavy rain, an Apollo truck was speeding along Westheimer. A large wake from the fast moving vehicle caught a lady broadside in the next lane. Her car drowned out and she called a garage to tow the car and dry out the spark plugs.

Nick got a call the next day that began "your old damn Apollo truck drowneded out my car . . ." When Nick could finally get in a word he apologized. "I'm so sorry for your inconvenience. I'm sure the truck was going much too fast and I will speak to the driver about it! What was the charge for fixing your car?" There was a pause at the other end. "Are you saying you would pay that?" "Of course, give me your address and I'll mail you a check."

Soon after the check arrived the lady called back clearly surprised. "But I told you the charge was only $25.00 and this is a check for $50.00." "Yes I sent you the extra amount for all the trouble we caused you and I really chewed out that driver!" "You are the nicest man—and I hope you just sell lots to paper to everybody!" Nick thanked her and hung up.

One of Nick's favorite sales pitches was, "we back order about 2% of our paper supplies and we always deliver the following day. However, you will never know whether or not I'm telling you the truth until you give me an order."

Favorite saying regarding human nature: "everyone wants to work for a good organization but they don't want to get organized because it exposes the fact they are not working like they should."

Cardinal rule: don't lie to customers as in "your order is on the truck." Sometimes potential customers would lie to him. "Your price is too high, I'm paying $—." Often the price they would name was lower than Apollo's cost and he knew they were not being truthful. Nick never bothered with those accounts. He knew if he quoted a price they would use it to get a lower one from their current supplier—usually a friend.

Cardinal rule #2: "If you have to have an answer right now, it's no!" #3 "If you are simply going in to an account and cutting prices, that is not selling!"

For nearly twelve months in a row in 1984-85 Apollo lost money. Obviously this could not continue. Instead of laying anyone off, all employees including Nick and Joe, took a 6% pay cut. About nine months later salaries were restored to their former level. All employees worked harder and faster during this time to restore the lost wages. In the beginning someone on the sales force suggested laying off some truck drivers since they were idle with nothing to deliver. "You're the reason they are idle," Nick retorted. "Go out and sell something so they will have something on those trucks.!"

In spite of the long hours or maybe because of them, a good chemistry and enthusiasm developed among the group. They shared stories about the day and helped each other with accounts. They began to believe Nick's mantra, "working at this company is like winning the medal of honor."

Apollo Paper Company was started in a 2000 sq ft warehouse at 1401 Greengrass. It was located in the back end of an already existing business. As named in chapter one: Jane Mock ran the office, Leon Jarmon, the warehouse and A J Courville and Ralph McSpadden were the outside salesmen. During the early years three office girls three salesmen and a purchasing agent were added. After two years they expanded to an office and warehouse of their own on Fairway Park Drive.

THE NEW OFFICE ON FAIRWAY PARK DRIVE

Ed Hollingsworth Apollo's first purchasing agent, loved the Alabama Crimson Tide in the Bear Bryant days. If his team lost on Sunday it would be a sure thing that Ed would not be at work on Monday.

He was very meticulous in his habits. To illustrate: he had a particular place he kept his aspirin supply. He would open the box take out the bottle, remove the cotton, take the pill or pills and replace everything in the same exact order. He was just as painstaking in his recordkeeping. Ed kept track of each order, exact size, amount and day ordered. He had kept these for many years. He also possessed a phenomenal memory and could "cube" trucks and/or box cars. For those of us who are not familiar with this terminology, it meant he knew the exact size of each piece of merchandise and the number of cubic feet in each truck. The total pieces would then exactly fit in the truck or box car as the case might be. Prior to Apollo, Ed had been at Century Paper Co for nineteen years. Nick recognized his unique abilities and spent many evenings discussing business problems with him. To this day Nick lists Ed as the "smartest man I have ever known."

Today no one has to cube rail cars because they are no longer in use. In the first few years several Apollo suppliers would not ship by truck. They preferred rail transportation exclusively. This meant that the warehouse on Greengrass and later on Fairway Park Drive relied heavily on accessible rail siding.

Another one of Nick's early employees was Roland Rollins. Nick described him as one of the best pure salesmen he ever hired. Early in his career Roland was one of the stalwarts of Apollo. He seemed to be the whole package: neat, handsome, artistic and met people well. He designed the company's first brochure. It was three years before Roland knew he could sell below the "book price." Apparently nobody cared. Men and women customers alike wanted to buy from him.

When the company first started, business cards were handwritten. Roland was among the first to receive a printed business card. Nick and Roland picked up his new cards as they were out making calls. Assuming they were correct they gave one to the first customer. "Roland Collins," she read aloud. "No, not Collins, Rollins!" Roland corrected. Long after the cards had been correctly reprinted Roland was still called "Collins." To Nick's intense disappointment Roland died at an early age and never truly reached the potential Nick envisioned for him.

Like Ed Hollingsworth before him another employee that was of great help to Nick was Greg Raindl. Greg by his own admission "does not play well with others." In other words Greg is task oriented. He was Ed's equal in banking and money matters.

Nick had lunch with him and a mutual friend and hired him on the spot. Greg's former job was with a large public accounting firm. Nick later was to say Greg did all the things he "had not a clue" how to do. He also negotiated and oversaw the construction of the warehouse built on highway 290 and again when they moved to beltway 8. Nick confesses that Greg had to show him where his office was when construction was completed.

Perry Woolery was hired away from a good customer, always a risky move. Early on when Nick was still making a lot of calls he tried to call on Perry. Each time he would have to go find him because although Perry was the buyer, he was never in his office. As he saw Perry time after time running through the warehouse he thought, "this is the hardest working man I've ever seen. I'm going to hire him!" Perry never disappointed. In all his Apollo years he was always the same hard working guy.

After Perry had been with Apollo for some time he came to Nick figures in hand, requesting to buy a tow motor. "Do you need one, Perry?" he asked as he threw the figures in the trash, "if you do then go buy it!"

Charles Roche came from a job at Century Paper Co and was a friend of Ed Hollingsworth. He and Perry were both former Marines and that was fine with Nick. Perry and Charles together ran the warehouse one for each shift. They had a mutual respect and worked well together. Joe tried to promote Charles to operations manager and insisted he wear a shirt and tie and work inside. Charles was miserable. "I want to sweat!" he complained to Nick. Realizing he was not happy in his new position, they returned him to 'happiness' in the warehouse.

Nancy Kroeger was working for an oil and gas equipment co. Nick had first met her at the Murray Rubber Co when she was their buyer. They had kept in touch and one day he asked her to meet him for lunch. He hired her and asked if she would start a telemarketing division for Apollo. She said, "what's telemarketing?" He replied he didn't know either. Nancy said she would try—and so began the experiment with phone solicitation.

She was later transferred to head the purchasing department. Her inside sales department was doing three million dollars annually. By that time apparently they both had figured out what telemarketing was. When Nick sold the company he recommended that Nancy be put in charge of the Houston division.

Wayne Barham worked for East Tex Motor Freight. Ralph McNabb at the Sealed Air Corporation had interviewed Wayne for a job with them. Out of one hundred applicants only two guys were left: Wayne and Joel Winston. Ralph said he could hire only one, and planned to hire Joel, but the other was just as well qualified. He suggested that Nick talk to Wayne feeling that "he would be good for Apollo."

When Nick called Wayne he found he wasn't ready to leave East Texas. They had promised him some incentives to stay. He wanted to give it some time; a year. Nick wrote Wayne's name on his calendar and called him exactly a year later. Well, Wayne did things work out like they said?" Silence. "Well, probably not. Can you come to my office tomorrow?" Wayne agreed and Nick hired him immediately.

Like those who are comfortable with each other Apollo people were constantly teasing or playing practical jokes on each other. Wayne had been with the company for quite some time when this happened. It was summer and Houston was in the midst of a drought. Nick looked out the window and said, "wow, it's really coming down out there! It's flooding!" He knew Wayne had left the windows down in his car. Wayne fell over a coffee table in his haste to get to his car to close the windows. He came back in and said to Nick, "you dirty dog!" About two weeks later Nick nudged Wayne and said, "Wayne, it's snowing in Conroe."

Gay Nevill Griffin called on Nick representing a large hotel chain. She was in charge of selling meeting rooms in the hotel. The room was free. All the company bought was the breakfast meal. Nick pointed out that they already had a room where they held meetings. "But how about evenings?" she persisted. After work alcohol was served by the hotel. Nick said he would get back to her in two days. He was looking at her as a possible hire and wanted to see how she would follow up. Sure enough two days later she called back. She didn't make the sale for the hotel but she landed a new job.

After Gay had been with the company for a while a personal crisis arose and she pursued Nick down the hall. She had received her "golden rods." These sheets told the employee based on their sales, how much they would be paid that month. She discovered what she perceived as an accounting error and wanted Nick to correct it. He told her he had "ten things on his mind" and would get to it when he could. She followed him out to the warehouse and back trying to explain the error. He finally had more than he could stand, took the papers and flung them to the floor. They scattered everywhere. As she bent down to pick them up he gave them a kick. She later told Ivan her husband at the time, he had kicked so close to her head that she could "smell his shoe polish!" Ivan told her she should have let him kick her—"and then we would own Apollo Paper Co."

APOLLO RELOCATES FROM FAIRWAY PARK TO
HIGHWAY 290.

Among those who labored so ably to make Apollo successful were: Martha McFarland, Judy Bell, Sonja Huerta, Mary Bond, Venetia Skelton, David Taylor and Carl Cormier. Cathy Wingo made a very significant contribution.

Nick often came home singing the praises of Cathy. It seemed nothing was too time consuming or too large an obstacle for her to overcome. On one occasion she had minor surgery—and returned to work that same day.

This story circulated about Carl Cormier and Gay. They had driven into the parking lot of a closed restaurant at 3:00am along highway 290. They decided to turn up the music, get out of the car and dance in the parking lot.

This attracted the attention of the policeman on duty. "We just decided to dance," they allegedly said to the officer. Since they were not breaking any laws he said "have a nice evening!" and drove off.

If Woody Benson was the "good Samaritan" of Apollo (his story appears on the next page,) Carl Cormier was Apollo's chef. He was already famous, with Nick, because he arrived on Thursday mornings at 5:00am, in order to place a special box order. He specialized in south Louisiana cuisine. "Bow dan" and gumbo were his specialties. If Apollo people brought food for some special occasion, his would always be the first to disappear. The title "handsome eligible bachelor" went to Gary Messer. To each Apollo function he brought a different beautiful girl—until Meredith who worked at the company caught his eye. They are now happily married with two sweet young daughters. Gary blossomed into an excellent salesman. He later confessed to Nick that all he learned in college was to count goose eggs in forestry class.

SEVEN YEARS LATER APOLLO MOVES TO BELTWAY 8.

The good Samaritan of Apollo Paper

Woody Benson, "Woo Woo" as he was affectionately called was the good Samaritan of Apollo Paper Co. Woody was one of those rare individuals who genuinely loves helping those in distress.

One day several years ago as he was out making sales calls, he happened upon a strange sight. A hearse with a flat tire was parked on the side of the road. The driver was surveying the damage as Woody drove up. "Can I help you?" The driver explained his problem. It seems he had a coffin in the back of the hearse that contained a body. He had been on the way to the funeral home at the time the flat occurred. Cell phones had not yet been invented.

Woody was driving a van. He had the idea that perhaps if they flattened the two back seats the coffin would fit. He immediately set to work. When the space was prepared he and the driver removed the coffin. They pushed and shoved mightily to force it into the back end of the van. It just wouldn't fit.

At this point in the story most of us would have offered our profound apologies and expressed optimistic hope that other help would somehow come soon. We would have then driven off feeling we had done all we could.

To Woody Benson this was only a minor setback. The two men unloaded their cargo from the van and deposited it beside the hearse. By this time they were both sweating profusely under the unforgiving Texas sun.

They had already removed their suit coats some time ago.

Woody's next challenge was to entirely remove the two back seats in his vehicle. Sometime later the seats were stacked on the growing pile beside the road. This time the coffin slid easily into the van. The driver looked at his watch in dismay, then he and Woody drove as fast as they safely could to the funeral home.

As they entered the funeral grounds the strains of "Nearer My God to Thee" could faintly be heard—probably being played for the third or fourth time. Two men in shirt sleeves eagerly approached the van. No, it was not the vehicle they had been expecting, but at this point any type of conveyance was reason for hope.

As the van was opened and the hoped-for "treasure" was unloaded, smiles of relief were on every face. Here was an incidence of a man who could legitimately claim, posthumously, of being late to his own funeral!

Woody and those like him will probably never receive a medal or have a speech given in their honor, but they are the salt of the earth—the ones who come along side and bring help and joy to us all. Thanks, Woody!

To catch a thief (thieves)

It has been said if thieves would apply themselves to honest work using the creativity they employ in stealing, they would make excellent employees.

Along with honest excellent employees at Apollo Paper there have been some excellent thieves hired as well. The Dallas office was located in a warehouse complex. The space next door was vacant. There were no cement walls separating one space from another in case a tenant wanted to expand. Only sheet rock separated the various slots.

Six foot bundles of microfoam were stored along the wall separating Apollo's space from the one next door. As time went by it became obvious that merchandise was somehow disappearing from the warehouse. Some enterprising thief knocked a hole in the sheet rock hidden from view behind the foam. Mystery solved. Since the warehouse next door was vacant it was an easy matter to come back after work and retrieve the stolen goods. During the day those involved would throw small items (toilet tissue, paper towels and tapes of all kinds) through the hole then cover it with the foam. These items could then be easily sold to friendly sources with no questions asked.

Less imaginative but no less effective was the idea some thieves devised of throwing items in the dumpster during working hours. They would then cover the stolen goods with waste materials. Since there was no protective fence around the dumpster, they could come back and pick their loot out of the trash when it was dark.

Another discovered plot was to load the truck with extra products. The driver would make his stops and deliver the correct amount to each account. However in between scheduled customers, he made some unscheduled stops and unloaded the excess stuff.

In one case stealing became so severe that it was obvious a large group had to be involved. In this instance Nick hired a private detective agency to work on the case. First Perry and Charles were alerted. The agency was to send out one of their men and Perry and Charles were told to hire him. The man's job was to observe, blend in and gain the acceptance of those being watched. He would then send a report to the agency, who would in turn report to Nick nightly. Over time the agent was able to learn how the thieves operated and the name of each one involved.

The time came to close the net. One suspected driver would be followed first by one vehicle then at designated points, different cars would take over. Cell phones were not in use yet but the men would keep in touch by two-way radio. Stops were made at paint and body shops (not Apollo customers) and masking tape for painting cars was dropped off. Motels bought a good grade of toilet tissue for a cheap price. On and on the driver went totally oblivious to what was about to transpire.

It was discovered that one of the offenders had stolen merchandise stashed in his garage. Unlike the others he had kept his portion and was planning to distribute it later. Escorted by a detective he was forced to return the goods he had taken. This was to be the only part of the loss that Apollo recovered.

The detective asked Nick if he wanted them sent to jail. Nick replied "absolutely." Then he inquired if Nick or other employees ever worked late at night or on Saturday. Of course they did. He suggested that perhaps Nick might want to reconsider. Some or maybe all of the men had fathers and/or brothers who might take revenge for his sending "little son or brother" to jail. He warned Nick he would have to watch his back from then on. Faced with this possibility, Nick decided to fire them and let them go their way.

Management also got their "slice of the pie." About half way through our list of departed and unlamented Dallas managers was Chuck. Everyone after Chuck had to be considered a winner no matter how inept their performance. While ordering lumber to build racks for the warehouse, he ordered enough extra wood to build decking around his own swimming pool. Then he used Apollo's labor to construct his project. Although there's no evidence to support it, he probably used company funds to construct the pool as well.

Chuck as no one before him established a new low. He also devised a way to steal and resell pool chemicals. He would order the chemicals through Apollo have the company pay the bill, then confiscate them for his own purposes.

His main objective was to sell the chemicals to his fellow employees. Many of them also had swimming pools. He sold them cheap so the employees were happy. Chuck pocketed the money and chemicals for his own use so he was extremely happy . . . and the company paid the bill. Nice! Although Chuck's tenure was short it was certainly memorable.

Until now the thievery would be described as being of the inside variety. Now we progress to a truly baffling "outside" case. This occurred one Monday morning in the early nineties. It was 7:30am and the trucks were loaded and ready to go. As the first man prepared to get in his truck he made an amazing discovery. Not only were the truck tires stolen, but the rims as well. Only the axles remained! As each of the twelve drivers reached his truck he reported the same thing—no wheels!

It was necessary to not only call the police but all the customers as well. They had to tell them that their expected delivery would not be arriving this day. The remainder of the day and part of the next, was spent frantically trying to find tires and rims to get back on a normal delivery schedule.

How could this have happened? The trucks were protected by a Cox fence topped with razor wire. Upon closer examination the invaders had used wire cutters on the fence, rendering the razor wire useless. They simply rolled back the fence then rolled out the loot. It was a very simple operation but, as with most crimes, left complete chaos in its wake. They were never caught.

One "outside" case may have been apprehended we're not sure. This took place in the mid to late nineties. On Thanksgiving eve of that year Apollo had thirteen windows shot out by drive-by shooters. On Thanksgiving eve exactly one year later the same thing happened. Again thirteen large plate glass windows were shot out. Each time it was necessary to nail up plywood sheets until the new windows could be installed.

A few days after the second incident some people were apprehended shooting out windows on Houston's southwest freeway. Since these incidents were never repeated we wondered if the group that was arrested were *"our friends!."*

CHAPTER 5

PRIVATE LIVES

Our first real home was in southeast Houston near Hobby Airport. Nick found our house one day after working graveyards at Champions. He was so excited for me to see it. Fortunately he has good taste and I too loved the house. The time had come to sign our first big obligation as a couple. We swallowed hard and with sweaty hands, signed "Morris and Beverly Nicholson." We obligated ourselves to pay $15,950.00 within thirty years. Now we could move from the garage apartment! Both of our children were born in this first house.

We loved the Farrar family who lived next door. They had two daughters, Dottie and Diane. They were both baton twirlers and had a room full of trophies to prove it. Malone, their father had to build an extra room on the house to accommodate them. The room was filled to capacity.

When the girls were out practicing in their driveway cars would sometimes run up over curbs while watching them. Dottie had won the title of "Miss Majorette of America" and Diane was just as talented. Besides talented, they were both very attractive as well. Their mother Rene made all their costumes. I saw some of them and they were beautiful!

Nick ever the competitor, found a lawn farther down the street that was an example of how he wanted his lawn to look, only naturally he wanted his yard to look better. He began yard work with a vengeance, setting his sights on a sago palm. After carefully saving for weeks, he painfully parted with the purchase price of $5.00 and brought home his prize.

The next step was to build up his lawn with St. Augustine grass. This turned out to be much more difficult than merely buying a plant. He ordered a large dump truck of sand (16 yards.) With no wheelbarrow and having only a shovel, it took him two complete days, after graveyards to spread the sand. By the time we had owned our third house Nick thoroughly hated St Augustine grass. At the end of summer he found through experience it usually turned brown with chinch bugs.

NICK DISPLAYS HIS FISH

After the ordeal of spreading sand and building a mat on the lawn, Nick turned his attention to other details. He planted a Queen's Vine intending it to climb some heavy twine he strung from top to bottom to form a trellis on the outside brick wall. Daily he watched anxiously as it inched its way up the twine and anticipated the day it would begin blooming.

Dottie and Diane saw how he watched the vine every day and decided to hasten things along. They bought several pink flowers and attached them to the vine. Nick could hardly contain his excitement until close examination proved them to be plastic. He knew right where to find the conspirators.

Betty Humphries, our neighbor on the other side would watch my car drive in from work and immediately ring the doorbell to ask to come over, smoke and drink coffee. She was a "people person" and had done all her daily work by the time I arrived home at 3:00pm. Usually her visits were welcome, but sometimes not. I had been up since 4:30am.

One year Betty and I planned a surprise birthday party for Nick. He bore it with good humor but I was later to learn that he did not like surprises. People who carefully plan for *everything* don't usually enjoy being surprised.

Malone had a garage full of tools and machines that he used constantly. When he wasn't doing yard work Nick would sit with Malone in his garage and listen to stories about the 2nd WW in the Pacific. Malone had made a career of the Navy and he and his family had lived overseas for extended periods of time.

One evening we invited Rene and Malone over to the house for coffee. I was in the last month of carrying out first child, Mark. I was still working at Braniff and by evening I could have laid my head down on the table and slept. Nick couldn't understand how I could be so rude to our guests as I sat there numbly nodding and trying to smile. He was glaring at me and kicking me under the table to keep me awake. Rene and I talked later and she completely understood the problem since she had two children of her own.

We dined out one evening with the Farrars. We had a "buy one get one free" coupon so we celebrated. That evening I ate shrimp stuffed with crab meat. The next morning I arose as usual to get ready for work. Things began to turn black and I immediately called in sick. Nick was aware something was very wrong when I slumped into a chair by the phone. There were other symptoms. My eyes and lips were swelling and my throat began to close.

Our car at the time was a nineteen sixty Thunderbird. These cars were designed with a large "hump" in the middle of the back seat. I remember trying vainly to lie down comfortably over this hump as Nick sped to the emergency room. Once there I upchucked the contents of my stomach and was thereby saved from having my stomach pumped. After the removal of the offending food both Nick and I felt better. Following a shot of medicine designed to reduce swelling, Nick took me home and put me to bed. I had completely recovered by the next day.

Years later our two families reconnected. The three of them had hardly aged. As noted in the introduction Dottie passed away at an early age. Diane looked as though she had just stepped out of her high school yearbook, although she was sixty by this time. Malone and Rene in spite of health issues still looked good.

Ceramic class provided a plethora of accessories for our new house. I still remember Billie Rhoades and the classes Nick's sister Ann and I attended. At one such class an old girlfriend of Nick's showed up. From all reports she had been quite serious about marrying him. While he was in the Corps she had spent a lot of time ingratiating herself to Nanny. He assured me he was never serious about her. I'll never know because we made a pact when we married. "You don't talk about old boyfriends and I won't talk about old girlfriends." For the most part we've kept that promise.

Apparently Jerry came to see what the person who married Nick looked like. I couldn't blame her. I was just grateful our positions were not reversed.

The good ole days

While waiting to find Nick, I worked at Braniff Airways. It was an interesting and well-paying job. I was a ticket agent and worked in the lobby of Hobby Airport checking in passengers for flights. All tickets were handwritten.

Occasionally we were privileged to meet celebrities. Edith Head showed us the jeweled ten gallon hat that had been presented to her at Neiman Marcus. I chatted with Carl Bendtson who was president of Nick's company, Champion Paper. I also talked with two different presidents of Grinnell College from my hometown in Iowa. One of them (President Bowen) hospitably invited us to drop over to see him the next time we were in Grinnell.

John Unitas and I had a brief—and funny—conversation. As he checked in he asked, "would you like to come along?" Usually I just passed off such remarks knowing they were not seriously intended. However I was newly married, and bristled at the innocent comment. I retorted, "well, I'd rather go with my husband!" As he stomped off he said, "well, I'd rather go with my wife!" It was only then I looked at his name. The poor man was only trying to make conversation thinking "<u>surely</u> this person knows who I am!" Even I as a football illiterate knew his name. Sorry John!

One time Oral Roberts looking dead tired from overseas meetings took time for a very meaningful (to me) chat about the work in which he was involved.

A short thin little man checked in with me one day. He wore a brimmed hat a small bow tie and a light yellow shirt with tiny pin stripes. He would easily be overlooked in a room full of people. "Do you know who you just checked in?" someone asked. I looked at the name. Newly arrived from Iowa, Clint Murchison, Sr. meant nothing to me. "No," I truthfully replied. Mr. Murchison it seemed owned only one acre of land, a very small amount for Texas. The only difference was, it was in downtown Fort Worth. I was to learn that this was true of the entire Murchison family; quality people who lived simply and didn't flaunt their wealth.

One group of guys who were talented singers and guitar players (but not well known) broke out their instruments and sang a whole concert for us agents during the time their flight was delayed.

Sonny Liston, world heavyweight champion at that time checked in with me. He looked to be on drugs or alcohol or both. He probably should have been training instead of traveling around the country. I told him my husband was a boxing fan and would he please sign an autograph for me? Without a word he pointed at the skinny little man who was with him. I smiled, shook my head and offered him a pen and paper to sign. After asking, I was afraid I had embarrassed him. Perhaps he couldn't sign his name! However he did. I got it just in time. His next bout was against Cassius Clay—"who floated like a butterfly and stung like a bee"—and took the title from him.

Kay Starr, a popular singer in the 50's was very personable. She told this story about herself. This woman apparently looked her up and down (in her expensive full-length fur coat) and remarked, "I don't know who you are, but you must be *somebody* to be wearing a coat like that!"

Other celebrities, with names now forgotten, conversed with us now and then. These were slower times with fewer passengers to board. Now the airlines have a "cattle car" mentality and those who can afford it fly their own private air transportation.

Airlines in those days sold service. If a flight or flights were going to be delayed the following morning, the night crew in reservations phoned each passenger who would be affected and informed them of the new departure time. The early morning flights out of Hobby Airport were often delayed because of fog that rolled in from the coast the night before. If there were those connecting to other flights in Dallas, Chicago or wherever, reservationists would "protect" them on later connecting flights. Also the much maligned airline food looks pretty good in comparison to today's airline cuisine—NONE.

Braniff Airways declared bankruptcy a few years after I departed. The exact reason or reasons may never be determined. Their advertising slogan may have helped, "if you've got it, flaunt it!"

I personally believe I know of one other. Braniff while I was there had exclusive rights to the Houston/Dallas route. There were never any directives sent down from the top to remind us that these travelers paid our salaries and we were to treat them with consideration and respect. All of us had checked in passengers who angrily remarked that when another carrier began operating between Houston and Dallas, "they would never fly Braniff again." Of course, in time that day arrived. The following story is inexcusable in any case. Courtesy should be shown to everyone.

Ed, after apparently listening to a passenger's complaint said with a smirk, "if you don't like it take a bus!" I was appalled. This response should have cost him his job or at least a reprimand. Besides Ed, there may have been others who had this same attitude.

Dick Haymes vs Braniff Airways

I worked on Braniff's evening shift one night a week. This was early in my airline career and soon after, I started working days exclusively.

This particular evening who should appear at my counter to check in but Dick Haymes. Dick was a contemporary of Frank Sinatra's and rivaled him in popularity at the peak of his career. He had a remarkable singing voice and had starred in several movies by this time. His love life had also been remarkable having been married to Rita Hayworth and Ava Gardner and who knows how many more. Dick was now on the down side of his career. His voice was still okay, but he had aged as a result of his lifestyle. Rumored to be an alcoholic he died a few years after this incident.

Dick had however just been featured on TV a few nights previously. It was fresh on my mind when he checked in. "Oh, Mr. Haymes." I gushed, "you were <u>wonderful</u> on the TV special this past week!" He was gracious because by that time he was running low on fans and welcomed any kind word. "Gate 7," I announced and added that his flight would be called shortly.

After the flight had left—guess who, and his female companion, came back to the counter to inquire when his flight would leave. It had been the last scheduled flight of the evening. To my dismay I discovered that the flight, which always departed from gate 7, had left from gate 10 this evening!

I was abjectly apologetic realizing I had made a mistake and caused him to miss his flight. Pat Powers, the assistant station manager, gave me a murderous look that said, "shut up and let me handle this!" As it turned out everyone had been given the wrong information. It was posted on the board as gate 10, but no one bothered to inform us agents. We were all so used to a gate 7 departure that no one bothered to check the board.

Mr. Haymes and his companion were forced to pay for their own over-night accommodations since everyone else had found the correct gate and boarded the flight. It was presumed from his reputation that he and his friend camped at gate 7 and opened a bottle . . .

That incident cured me. I never gushed over a celebrity again.

UNFORGETTABLE . . . RICHARD, DALE AND JEAN

Dick Kramer and I had two things in common. We were both Yankees, although he was considered more of a Yankee than I was. He came from Pittsburgh—and was considered an Eastern Yankee while I came from the Midwest. The Midwest apparently was more acceptable. It's hard to realize now, but Texas was still fighting the Civil War when I moved to Houston. (Not really, but sentiments still ran deep. Restrooms, drinking fountains and restaurants were all still segregated. The Confederate flag was still seen in many places.)

The second thing Dick and I had in common was that we both worked for Braniff Airways. Although we were never close friends, Dick had such a great sense of humor that we all loved him. He was however very shy and well on his way to becoming a confirmed bachelor. At the close of one work day he sighed, "well, I guess I'll go up and smell Eunice's perfume and go home." Although gorgeous, Eunice was safely married so she was not so intimidating.

Each day after work Dick went home to watch his daily soap opera. The characters on the soap became like family to him. I still remember one of the character's names on the show, "Sarah Carr." He talked about the show continuously and everyone at Braniff knew Sarah Carr. One day to Dick's utter shock and disbelief they "killed" Sarah Carr in the script. He mourned her loss for several days saying dejectedly, "they killed Sarah Carr!"

He was often gently teased about his Pennsylvania roots. The claim was made that Houston was "where it's at" and nothing good ever came from Pittsburgh. To silence his critics, one morning Dick turned over a breakfast roll and pretended to discover the words "made in Pittsburgh" on the back.

My particular friend at Braniff was Jean Crockett. She insisted that I come with her to a rehearsal of the Sweet Adelines, a female barbershop singing group. (The group was trying to get the Imperial Sugar Co. to sponsor them. They wanted to call themselves "the Imperial Sugars.") My protest that I was tone deaf was of no avail. I went just to prove my point—and she never asked again.

Her particular talent was that she was able to wake up late and dress in her car on the way to work from across town. These were the days of tight-fitting girdles so it was quite an amazing feat! As far as I know she had never wrecked the car.

After working with him fifty years ago Dale Elmore who lives in this area turned up in the same Sunday school class with Nick and I. Not surprisingly we have both changed in appearance after all these years. I remember Dale's golden wavy hair which went the way of Nick's blonde wavy hair. Hair has a way of disappearing just when we need it most. Although I still have my hair it has changed from the dark brown of Braniff days to probably snow white. (Actually I have no idea what color it is as I haven't seen its natural state in years.) This fact is nicely disguised by an ash blonde rinse thanks, Loreal!

Except for his hair Dale has not changed a bit. He's still full of conversation, laughter and fun. He remembers his days at Braniff with gusto and will recount them to anyone who is interested.

Speaking of Sunday School (now called Life Group at Humble Area First Baptist Church) we have an excellent teacher, Jim Wisenbaker (who is sometimes assisted by Steve.) Jim's wife, Char is active in class projects. A testimonial to Jim's teaching is the fact that we have to get up at 6:00am to get to class. The days I arose at 4:30am to work for Braniff are OVER. Life goes much smoother when arising at 7:00am. One of Jim's favorite sayings, "if it ain't hurtin', it ain't workin'!"

I continually remind Ruth Billings that she has a job for life as class president. She has set the bar so high no one would attempt to follow Ruth. Each week she emails a newsletter sparked with humor regarding class functions and prayer needs.

Charlie and Mildred are our popcorn experts. Charlie is our vice president and Mildred also does the class booklets (phone #s, email and home addresses.) These people make us all feel loved and encouraged.

Melva is special to us. Although Melva, like the rest of us sometimes can't get her body to work as she would like, in spite of that is constantly on the go. There are so many members of our class worthy of mention—but these are our "stalwarts" the ones who make things go.

Our new pastor and his family, Barry Jeffries and wife, Gay, were the results of a two and a half year search. Everyone seems to agree that it was worth the wait. We're grateful our search committee didn't settle for just anyone because they became weary of the ordeal. We feel they found God's man and he was faithful to hear and answer the call.

Our former minister, Dr. Bruce Frank was also a treasure. He and Nick became friends and frequently lunched together. He was always telling Nick he should "write a book" and include some life experiences. Pastor Bruce was kind enough to send us CD's of each sermon series—but now he's on DVD and sends those! Thanks Pastor Bruce.

Remember those Houston Oilers?
The days of "love 'ya Blue"

In the early days of our marriage we were big Oiler fans. I have fond memories of going down to the Adams Petroleum Building with Nick to buy tickets. In those days, Braniff handled the special charter flights for the team. The first two years the Oilers were champions of the newly formed AFL.

Nick and I attended the longest game ever played up to that time. The opponent, who also unfortunately won, was the Kansas City Chiefs. I nearly miscarried Mark because of sitting at that game on a hard bleacher for far too long.

The most memorable game was against the Oakland Raiders. Nick and I wore long johns, coats, sweaters; anything warm we could get on our bodies. We sat with our backs against a concrete wall to protect us from the wind. None of it was enough! I recall I didn't undress for two days until I finally got sufficiently warm to change clothes. Also, I don't remember the score or who won that game immediately after it ended, let alone now. My only goal was to go home and get thawed out.

After the first two years, the rest of the league started catching up with the Oilers and games were not quite as fun. There were times that we as fans had to manufacture our own fun in the stands because it wasn't to be found on the field.

George Blanda, quarterback for the Oilers was colorful and good for several stories. This weekend he was not playing; perhaps out with an injury. Another quarterback whose name I mercifully can't remember was running the team. A trumpeter somewhere in the stands was entertaining the crowd with his music. Things were not going well on the field. Interception after interception was thrown and by this time the Oilers were well behind the opposing team. Then by some miracle the inept quarterback threw a pass for a touchdown. The guy on the trumpet belted out "everybody loves somebody sometimes!" a song made famous by Dean Martin and popular at the time. We all laughed and applauded the timely sentiment.

George too, had games where he couldn't seem to connect with his receivers—Oilers that is. His passes would too often find themselves in the hands of the other team. Often the crowd could be heard admonishing him: "throw to the blue, George, only to the blue!"

At another game a fan observed Charley Hennigan returning late from down field. The rest of the team had already lined up for the next play. He yelled, "don't tell Charley the play!" Again, there seemed to be more entertainment in the stands than on the field.

Besides being quarterback, George also kicked field goals and extra points. After he had kicked an extra point and was returning to the bench, an opposing lineman tackled him. George was not content with merely receiving a penalty on behalf of his team. As the offending player walked back to his huddle, George ran over and kicked him squarely in the seat of the pants! After that both benches emptied and there was bedlam on the field for awhile.

After Blanda was traded to Oakland, the Bum Phillips/ Earl Campbell era began. Bum was from the country complete with ten gallon hat and boots. He brought the down-home, "love 'ya Blue" flavor to the Oilers. During this period the city took the Oilers to its heart and the coach and players were loved and honored by all. During Bum's tenure it was agreed that the team truly overachieved.

Bum made popular the phrase "hold the rope" a country-ism that to him typified the teamwork he was trying to instill in his players. It became popular all over town. Ropes were even passed out during the playoffs.

Nick would see Bum on the golf course—still wearing his boots—with spikes adorning the bottoms of them.

Probably the beginning of the Oilers' demise could be traced back to the year Bud Adams (owner) fired Bum. The team never seemed to have the support of the fans after that and ended up moving to Tennessee.

Then as now, rowdy drunken fans could be a real nuisance. They always seem to be heard above everyone else. At one game a guy had consumed so much alcohol he had forgotten Bob Talamini's name. He was disgustedly yelling "stupid 61!"

Somewhere along the way our interest in the Oilers began to wane. As the players somewhat normal in size in the earlier years, began to seriously bulk up it changed the game for us. A short while after that an Oiler player was carried off on a stretcher. He sustained such serious injuries he was forced to retire from the game. Our enthusiasm also "took a hit" that day. Nick and I decided we should spend our money on a less violent sport.

Enter Rocket Mania

It took several years to transfer our loyalty from the Oilers to the Houston Rockets. In between we tried really hard to get interested in the Astros. We had some good seats available to us—at the Astrodome—but when the team moved to Enron Field (later renamed Minutemaid Park) it proved too much of a change for us. To create room for a larger number of desirable seats, they all had to be moved farther back from the field.

At one game in the Astrodome, Jeff Bagwell came to the on-deck circle which was located close to our seats. Apparently he was looking for sympathy as he said dejectedly, "I can't hit him!" meaning whoever was pitching at the time. At another game Craig Biggio tossed a ball to us around the screen. Former President George H. Bush was in attendance with (owner) Drayton McClain. Walt Chandler Nick's manager of Apollo, Dallas was there as our guest. Walt asked both the President and Drayton to autograph the ball for his son Ford.

Those were great evenings since it was possible to interact with some of the players. When they moved to Enron it was never quite the same.

About that time we began to notice the Rockets were starting to show some promise. That year they lost in the finals to the Boston Celtics in six games.

The following season play-off hopes were dashed before they began. Two starting players on the team were banned from the league for illegal drug use. Nevertheless we had become hooked on the team. They had potential and a few years later won two championships in a row from 1994-96. Houston became "clutch city" and our allegiance to the Rockets was firmly established.

We began attending Rocket games fairly regularly. The best seats available in the house on a regular basis were located in the "crow's nest" and best viewed with binoculars.

For one particular game we decided to splurge and buy $100.00 seats. They were located on the front row. (A $100 for a front row seat? I didn't realize until we got to the game the type of 'front row seat' I had purchased.)

In the meantime I told all my friends and even slight acquaintances "be sure to watch the Rockets as we had purchased front row seats and might be on TV!" If there had been such a thing as a cloak room at the "Summit" (where the games were held) that would have been where our front-row seats were located! I never realized how far from the floor the "front row" extended! The seats had a worse view than the crow's nest—you just didn't have to climb stairs.

Although we enjoyed the games, occasionally our interest would wander. Those little ant-like people running up and down the floor seemed so distant. We would often find ourselves people watching. We saw many friends seated in different places throughout the Summit. One night Nick noticed John Nelson seated in a front row seat close to the Rocket bench. Nick knew John from playing golf with him. Every time we came there was John. He *must* have season tickets Nick reasoned. It also looked as though he had several people in his party.

The next time Nick saw John at the golf course he asked about his tickets. He did have season tickets; four of them. John had these seats for twenty three years. Next question: would he sell two of them? Nick held his breath. It turned out John was retiring the next year and moving to Florida. We were only half-way home. The next question was whether the Rockets would allow a person to sell their tickets to another direct—or would the tickets have to be turned back into the office for those waiting to upgrade. We were "waiting to exhale" until we got the final okay. Only then were we jubilant when the Rockets ruled in our favor.

Sharing the bench with Yao Ming (sort of)

John did sell us the tickets and now probably someone in the Crow's Nest is watching us and plotting how to buy our tickets.

The Rocket games are now played at Toyota Center. It's a noisy, glitzy place. Lights flash around the floor. The "Rocket" launches at the start of each game with appropriate smoke and noise. Women, little more than girls, parade around the floor in brief, loud-colored outfits and Clutch, the team mascot comes in waving a "Houston Rocket" banner. You can count on that sequence every game before the presenting of the color guard and the singing of the National Anthem. The game that follows is rather anti-climactic after all that.

We have become friends with Patty Smith the woman who does TV broadcasting for the Rockets, the Texans and the Astros. A couple of years ago she interviewed us on TV. Our friends questioned us. Did you get "made up" for your appearance? Did they rehearse you? We told them "no" to both questions. She did tell us what she would ask and gave us a few minutes to decide what we wanted to say.

We never did get to see the interview. Quite a few recorded the game but later erased it! I for one am glad. Our friends were complimentary. I'd rather have their analysis than be faced with the actual reality!

One evening as we were seated in our "new" seats, I nudged Nick. "What do you suppose one hundred million Chinese would give to be sitting this close to their idol?" Yao Ming sat about ten feet away from us at the time.

Now that we have them, forty plus games each season becomes a very large time expenditure for one sport. We're stuck with them because if we fail to renew them someone has to die before seats like this become available again! Anybody want to buy some games?

CHAPTER 6

IT'S ALWAYS SAD To LEAVE

After a few years we found it necessary to move from our house on Reed Road. We loved our first house. It had wonderful memories and we had become good friends with our neighbors; leaving them was also hard. However, we had compelling reasons to leave. It is sufficient to say we were not prepared financially to relocate. After a lot of discussion, we decided to build a new house in west Houston.

Shirley Johnson was the decorating consultant employed by our builder, Paul McConnell and was also a new neighbor. Working with Shirley made our decisions much easier. Everything she suggested we knew was within our allowance and so we would readily agree. Neither Nick nor I had any decorating experience anyway, so It seemed best to take her suggestions. We chose everything for the house, down to and including the hardware knobs, in one afternoon. We thought, "why do people find this so hard to do? It isn't even time consuming." We were to find out differently on subsequent houses.

Next came the real challenge furnishing a house with minimal funds. All our "new" furniture came from flea markets and had to be refinished and re-covered. We made many of the decorative items ourselves. How successful were we? Judge for yourself. Our little daughter, Lynda, had been in the homes of her friends. Our house did not compare favorably with theirs. She asked a very pointed question: "are we poor?" Since she was pretty sure we were, she had brought along the money from her piggy bank to help us through the perceived crisis.

One night a fire started in our utility room. Nick awoke and said "I smell smoke!" This was amazing because our bedroom was at the front of the house and the utility room was located in the back. Also, Nick was working long hours and slept soundly. He dashed to the back of the house and opened the utility room door. A huge plume of smoke billowed out. There was little doubt that this was the source of the fire.

Earlier that day we had used linseed oil to clean our tile floors. The oily rags had been left on top of the dryer, the light left on and the door closed. Spontaneous combustion does occur! Unbelievably, there was no damage to the dryer. The paint was not even blistered. The Lord graciously provided a strong northerly wind that blew through the house. The following morning there was no smell of smoke anywhere. Psalm 121:3 says" He who keeps you will not slumber."

Still strapped for cash, we were faced with having to fence in our property. Lynda was starting to wander away from home. I would look outside expecting to see her but she was nowhere in sight. The search was on. Our subdivision, Walnut Bend was located on a treeless prairie. It would be a few years before we had some trees capable of blocking the wind and providing shade.

As I frantically ran from house to house looking for my wayward child I became aware of wind blowing my hair straight up and over my face. I'm sure I looked to the neighbors like a wild frantic person. A great first impression. At last a compassionate lady living on the next street found her and brought her home. She had probably been knocking on doors just as I had.

It became obvious that a fence was needed not only for Lynda but also for the dog. We somehow got together the funds and the fence gradually became a reality. Now we believed our problems would be ended.

After the fence had been completed I looked out one day to see the dog digging under the fence gate and Lynda squeezing between the bars! In a last desperate measure Nick put chicken wire across the gate and extended it down far enough that Lynda and the dog were at last secured.

A year later Nick started Apollo and our salary magically doubled. With a few extra dollars in our pocket we were ready to try our hand at redecorating. We bought some smoked mirrored tiles and Nick applied them to the walls of the entry hall. These had just become popular so we thought we were really on the cutting edge!

Never one to shy away from color I decided to indulge myself. In the guest bathroom I used lime green and dark blue a popular combination at the time. In Mark's room we went with red, white and blue. We used lime green, pink and yellow in Lynda's room.

The piece de resistance was to be the wallpaper in the hall which I envisioned would tie it all together. It had lime green, yellow, orange and white bold stripes. (How could we possibly have walked up and down the long narrow hall several times a day and not become violently ill? What was I thinking?) Fortunately our Divine Decorator overruled this disastrous decision.

Nick tried in vain to apply the wallpaper to the wall. It just would not "apply." It looked like some slap-stick comedy routine. He would roll it up the wall and it would roll back down. Finally after the third or fourth try he admitted defeat. "I can't understand why you had so much trouble with this paper. It's one of our best grades," said the store clerk when we returned it. After much head scratching, he agreed to swap it for another paper. I could barely hide my disappointment when Nick returned with the second wall covering. It had all the right colors but the stripe was small and muted.

This paper went on the wall beautifully and I wish we had photographed the finished project. It would have to rank among our most successful endeavors. After adding a credenza and candleholders it looked good! It also probably saved us a large Pepto-bismol bill.

Our opera singer next door

The Beal family lived next door. Lynda and Whitney were the first to get acquainted. Whitney was a year younger than Lynda. She was about 6 and Lynda 7 years old at the time. Since Whitney was enrolled in ballet we enrolled Lynda as well. They became good friends and Lynda spent the night at the Beal's house. Now it was Whitney's turn. She wasn't sure she wanted to come but evidently Lynda persuaded her. Here she came at bedtime with her blanket and bear. Around ten o'clock we heard this little voice pitifully pleading, "can I go home?" Nick escorted her next door, grateful she lived so close and not somewhere across town. It was decided to wait until the following year for another sleep-over.

Kay and I also became friends. We learned she was a piano teacher and sang with the Houston Grand Opera. Sometimes in midmorning we could hear her warming up her voice—like a mini concert. Delightful.

The pastor of our church was considering teaching a neighborhood Bible study. Kay and I worked together to canvas the surrounding neighbors to see if there was an interest. There was and we began a weekly study. Pastor Cheek taught us for several months.

About this time a situation developed in our church that made him feel he should leave. He had also reached retirement age and these two factors together prompted the decision. Of course as his students we knew in advance of his decision. It was a sad time for us and the church because he had been a very loving "leader of the flock."

To help soften the blow, with the pastor's permission, I invited Kay to sing for us at this last service. She was a member of another church but agreed to come. She sang the beautiful song, one of my favorites "I walked today where Jesus walked." What a shame she couldn't have come under happier circumstances. At the close of the service the pastor made his announcement.

Outside the church after the service Nick was greeting Tommy, Kay's husband. They knew each other and had played golf a time or two. Trying to lighten a rather sad occasion Nick said, "I can't believe this, your old lady comes to sing at our church and our pastor quits!"

Our subdivision, was becoming too crowded for Nick. We both longed for more space for ourselves and the kids. On a trip north of Houston we discovered Kingwood. At that time it had a grocery store, drugstore and a filling station. Although thinly populated at the time, it would soon earn its title of "the fertile forest." Nick fell in love with the golf course and decided the longer drive would be worth it.

Moving on up—we thought

So we built "the house from hell," as we affectionately called it. It rained a lot that year. This should have told us something from the start. Only one contractor built contemporary houses in Kingwood (our choice of architecture at the time.) One of the first mishaps occurred when a worker's foot slipped off a beam and crashed through the ceiling.

Worse things were to follow. Another workman (or maybe the same one) was searching for the return air vent. He used a sledge hammer to knock a hole in the wall, only to find it wasn't there. Nick was present when it happened and ordered him to leave and not return. Next, men carrying carpet into the master bedroom tore the wallpaper off one wall.

One disaster was completely preventable. The man who planned to install the cultured marble innocently left the tub, the tub surround, etc. stored against the dining room wall. The painters arrived and were incensed because this prevented them from finishing their work. They solved the problem by painting the cultured marble and then the rest` of the room. The marble installer was understandably upset when he returned.

Among other annoyances, the clothes washer drained water into the master bathroom. There was a limit of two appliances that could be in used at one time in the kitchen. More than two would trip the circuit breaker. The outside of the house was painted the wrong color and the open atrium in the center of the house flooded. One day just before we were to move in, I flipped the light switch rapidly off and on twice in a row. Who knows why. The result: every circuit in the house was blown out! Finally the mirror covering one whole wall in the dining room collapsed and broke in pieces and after we had been in the house for a while, mold began to grow in Mark's room.

I will have to accept blame for one disaster. Remember my love of color? I decided to use the intense yellow color from the kitchen wallpaper for the utility room walls. The painter reported it was "like painting the inside of an egg!" We ended up using a quieter pink instead.

When at last the house was finished Nick recalls they left concrete covering parts of the tile floor. Rather than calling them back, he spent the better part of two days cleaning the floors with muriatic acid. He felt it was a small price to pay to keep them out of the house for good.

It was Saturday morning and Nick and I had just awakened. It had been a hard week at work for Nick and I was celebrating the fact that no workmen would be coming back for a long time. We were in no mood to get out of bed. Then I remembered. I looked at my watch and yelled, "the Copps are coming!" Nick, barely awake, was trying to make sense of this statement. I was hastily dressing and called to him, "get dressed! Dan and Ruth Ann Copps are coming to hang some new shades—in this bedroom!" Relieved to know his wife hadn't totally lost it, he obediently dressed and together we made up the bed. Shortly thereafter the Copps made their appearance.

Would it surprise you to learn that our builder was forbidden to build any more houses in Kingwood? He had overextended himself (greed) and several homeowners were bringing lawsuits against him.

Almost as soon as we moved into that house I knew it wouldn't be long before we moved out. We ended up staying there six years and the people who bought it still live there. The house was actually in good shape when we moved because we had everything fixed by then.

Before we moved to the Twin Grove address in the Kings Forest II subdivision, I began a hobby that would consume both of us. We started making stained glass windows. I took a class in Humble and this launched our career. Before it ended we had produced thirty four projects. Building a new house provided the incentive.

NICK POSING WITH A STAINED GLASS PROJECT

While making sales calls Nick met Al Danforth who made huge stained glass windows for a living. That evening Nick announced that we must immediately change our methods of cutting glass. The method I learned was horse-and-buggy. Al was into production and his method in comparison was jet propelled. I balked at the change because I hated to start over. It was necessary however because my style of cutting was causing me to have tennis elbow.

One of our first projects was a large 36" diameter butterfly that we planned to one day have inserted in our upstairs window overlooking the street. Even though the house was still in the framing stage, we wanted to see how it would look when it was installed. We hoisted it into place and sat down to admire it. About a week later we were talking with friends. They were unaware that we were building a new house. In casual conversation they told us they had been out driving and saw this "amazing sight. This house was still under construction—but in the upstairs a stained glass butterfly had been installed!" We laughingly explained the "amazing sight."

As we settled into a routine I would design the pattern and usually buy the glass. We would then wrap the glass edges with copper foil and Nick would solder the design together. After several projects I suggested that he select the colors. He protested that he couldn't do that. "Why?" "I don't have the ability." What a revelation! I had an ability my superman husband didn't have.

At war with nature

We liked atriums open to the sky with a house built around it. After constructing two of these houses in a row we feel qualified to give this advice: don't build one! Scrap those plans! Atriums are meant to be a focal point but instead are money pits. In the first house we had shrubs and not much else. These were fine. In our second attempt where we intended to retire we decided to be more creative. We tried plants and wood decks, fruit trees and finally a pond with a waterfall. The last effort was most successful. Unfortunately at night winged creatures would swoop down and carry away fish. In time other uninvited guests would arrive.

The first squirrel apparently fell from a tree onto the roof and from there into the atrium. We thought he was "cute" and fed him. Soon via the squirrel hot line other freeloaders arrived. No more food was forthcoming! Nick provided a long, substantial tree limb to assist their departure. Since there was no more food one by one they left.

We have yet to figure out how an armadillo got in the atrium but somehow one did. At 3:00am one Saturday morning I awoke to hear a scratching noise coming from the atrium. I woke up Nick who was not at all thrilled at the sight. He was scheduled to tee off in a golf tournament at 7:00am that morning.

"I'll have to shoot him," he decided. The idea of shooting any animal—especially one that technically was inside the house—was abhorrent to me. "Well it isn't as though it's an endangered specie!" Nick declared. Although I knew Nick was a crack shot courtesy of the Marines, there were hazards. Plate glass windows almost completely surrounded the atrium. Only one small corner was protected by cedar boards. Nick chased it into that area and shot it in the head the only part of the armadillo that was unprotected. (We were also concerned about ricocheting bullets.)

The armadillo was not through wrecking Nick's sleep. It was a large creature and in its death throes managed to send rivers of blood over the windows and the ground underneath. Next task: haul in the hose and clean up all that blood. We overslept and Nick had to run to the first tee and start without even a practice swing. He hit his first shot wildly to the right and things, as they say, went downhill from there. The only positive thing was that we never again had an armadillo in the atrium.

NICK STRUGGLES AFTER A SLEEPLESS NIGHT

Before concluding this portion of the chapter, its necessary to relate some instances of God's care. One morning I went up in the attic to get Christmas decorations. "That's strange," I thought as I looked up and saw blue sky. What a shock. I realized lightening must have struck the house. Apparently it was recent because there was no water on the attic floor.

We had a friend Bill Anderson who had often helped us out in times of need. One time was when Nick and I were scheduled to leave on a trip to Switzerland. Nick had won this trip as a business award. Obviously we had to leave on the designated day or lose the trip. We discovered a raccoon in our attic and knew It would be disastrous not to take action before we left. Bill came to the rescue with a catch and release trap and triumphantly removed the varmint before our return. Everyone needs a Bill Anderson!

NICK AND I ON OUR WAY TO SWITZERLAND

So after the lightning episode my first thought was to call Bill. Our main concern was damage to the upstairs wiring. Bill came and to our intense relief reported no damage whatsoever! He also repairs roofs.

The next potential calamity involved the hot water heater in the attic. A repair man went into the attic to check out the problem. Soon after he went up he came back down. "You've got to see this!" Without explaining, and with a strange expression on his face, he led the way to the attic. There, above the heating unit, was a large area of the roof that was charred by a fire. Something or Someone had extinguished the blaze with no further damage. Thank You, Lord, for protecting us once again.

One night probably around 10:00pm, Nick was coming home from work. His car began to overheat. He was right at the Laura Koppe exit on highway 59 which is not a desirable place to be after dark. Nick was driving an expensive late model car and wearing a nice watch. He coasted up to a 7-11 store with steam rising from the radiator. There were three black men loitering in front of the store. There were no cell phones as yet and the pay phone in front of the store looked a mile away. How could he get to that phone to call AAA? As he pondered his situation, he dropped his watch in his sock for safe keeping.

He was startled to see someone approaching. "Can I help you, sir?" A young black man on a bicycle had ridden up to the car. Somehow Nick knew this was a person he could trust. He told him his dilemma and the man said, "go ahead and make your call. As long as I'm here they won't bother you." True to his word the man stayed until the wrecker came. When Triple A arrived Nick insisted that they load his new friend and his bicycle and take him home. "You may have saved my life," Nick said as he handed him a rather large bill. "I can't take that sir, it's too much." Nick insisted until at last he said, "all right. This way I can buy my little boy a bike." I've often thought of that night over the years and how different it could have turned out without God's protective hand.

Introducing special friends

In 1995 I made my first and only mission trip. My destination was Emerald, in the province of Queensland, Australia. I'm not sure I accomplished a lot to further the "kingdom," but I drank a lot of tea and made a lot of friends, some of whom I still email. The last two days were spent on R & R in northern Queensland in Cairns. There I met a lady also on the mission trip from South Carolina, Katie Watson. Katie was a widow and vowed, as I did, this would be her last mission trip! We had so bonded after those two days, I invited her to come visit me in Houston and she agreed to come. When I told Nick that she was coming he promised to be polite, but in the next breath declared he would probably be playing golf a lot while she was here.

When she arrived Nick was as charmed as I had been, and didn't mention golf again. She told us many stories about the churches she and Gill, (her husband) had started, mostly in the Northwest. Her favorite book in the Bible is Job. (Katie is one of the few people I know who has *read* Job, let alone listed it as a favorite.) She is proud of her accomplishment of memorizing the book of Hebrews—in eight years! Who wouldn't be proud of that? I'd probably wear a sign! I'm sure this is one reason why her mind is still so sharp at 93.

KATIE "ANSWERING THE PHONE" AT APOLLO

We are proud to have discovered a product that has proved invaluable to her. She has Macular Degeneration and was obviously limited in the studying and writing she could do. The machine is called a "video eye" and magnifies printing, etc., to a much higher power than a regular magnifying glass. Always a talented writer she has self-published four books and is working on a fifth. Amazing.

Katie is very interested in politics. She has "fired off" many letters of complaint to her congressional representative. One time a few years ago I called to get her opinion on the recent election. She wasn't available; she was still working at the polls.

Sometimes we have to wait our turn for a visit because Katie is off visiting one of her seven children and/or grandchildren (as well as great grandchildren. I must confess I have lost count of those!)

We have been friends for many years with Morris and Tracy Hatalsky. Morris joined the PGA Tour in 1973 and is now on the Champions' Tour. Tracy would often accompany him but after the children started school, not so often. We could count on seeing Morris at least once a year. He would stay with us when the Tour arrived in Houston. The first year they came, they drove a brown Dodge van with Divot and Kelly in tow. Divot and Kelly were their pre-family canines. The next year when we saw Morris and Tracy they had Daniel. Laura Rose arrived a couple of years later.

Nick recalls hearing a guy in the gallery at the Masters question, "who is that Mexican guy playing with Aioki?" Morris who is part Jewish, had dark handsome looks that the guy misinterpreted. Nick standing nearby corrected him. "That's Morris Hatalsky."

Paying the check at restaurants became a battle between Nick and Morris. This was at times almost a blood sport. They would occasionally give the waitress their credit card upon arrival. Other times one would excuse himself to go to the men's room, but in reality to find the server and pay the check first. At last after ten years or so they arrived at a truce. Tracy and I were glad.

In the early years, Daniel sometimes came too. Nick and Daniel especially bonded. Daniel loved the "Dukes of Hazard" when it was popular on TV and we would often hear him say. "alright you Duke boys, you're under arrest!" Athletic from birth, Daniel would throw a tennis ball against the garage door with such force his hair would fly up. This amused Nick and Morris no end. He and Daniel also made a few local fishing trips.

One year Morris and Tracy planned to attend a tournament which was an invitation only event. They asked permission to leave the children with us for the weekend. We were more than happy to comply. One day Nick was at work and I remember having the children in the car. They were quite young. I had to go back in the house for something and when I returned a few minutes later, both children were crying at the top of their lungs, perspiring and quite red in the face. I quickly turned on the air conditioner silently pleading, "please don't get sick before your parents get back!"

BABYSITTING DANIEL AND LAURA ROSE

In his late forties Morris had gotten burned out on golf. He took a couple of years off from the tour to design and build a golf course in the mountains overlooking Ashville, NC. It was part of a golf resort that has since become quite successful called "Trillium." A time away from the tour proved to be the tonic he needed. (The physical conditioning didn't hurt either.) He resumed his career this time on the Champions' Tour and was rewarded by being named Rookie of the Year!

Tracy and Morris are a great team. Tracy specializes in managing the family finances and investments. She is a petite blonde and of course he is tall and dark. They have exactly reproduced themselves in their children. Daniel is dark and Laura Rose is lighter haired. Facially they closely resemble their respective parents.

MORRIS AND TRACY—LOOKING GREAT TOGETHER

This past year Nick and I attended Daniel's and Alana's wedding in Florida. We also met an all-grown-up Laura Rose having completed an advanced degree, is now planning to pursue a career in government.

What would life be without kids?

You may be wondering what our children were doing during this time. They were busily growing up! As mentioned before, they were both born in our first house in southeast Houston. Following are a few stories that give some idea of the way they were as kids and later as adults. Nick and I love them very much. Of course parents are expected to say they love their offspring—but we're blessed to say we truly enjoy their company. We love and approve of those they married: Tony and Julie. Both couples have as their goal pleasing the Lord with their lives and the lives of their children.

Mark and Lynda both accepted Jesus as their Savior at an early age. It is definitely my opinion that this decision has given purpose and meaning to their lives—and those of their families. It has also helped us as their parents to avoid a lot of grief we might have otherwise encountered.

A story I recall about Mark's early childhood occurred one Saturday morning. He was about four years old. I was apparently running errands and Nick was keeping Mark and also trying to read the sports page. In order to read longer he was trying to involve Mark. It was football season and the Old Miss Rebels were scheduled to play Auburn University. Nick explained all that to Mark and showed him a picture of a football player. "Is that her, Daddy?" Mark inquired.

Lynda was fond of icees and her Dad never disappointed. She would wait for him to come home from work then race out to the driveway and ask, "did you bring me an icee?" (She pronounced it nicee.) Sometimes Nick would build the suspense by saying, "sweetheart they didn't have any icees today. "Oh," was the disappointed reply. Nick confesses he just wanted to see that big smile when he produced the icee and watch as she jumped for joy.

She coined such phrases as "pass the passing plate" in church and "last day morning" for yesterday. Her Aunt Ann told her she was giving her (Lynda) some basic pearls. She came home and showed us her new "basing" pearls. We treasure all these childish phrases (and Mark's too, just as all families do)

OUR LITTLE DARLINGS, MARK AND LYNDA

117

Lyn loved cars from an early age. Going to and from school she memorized the makes and license numbers of all the neighbors' cars. One day at the grocery store she remarked that "Mrs. Ford is somewhere here in the store." "How do you know?" "I saw her car in the parking lot." Sure enough we soon caught up with her a couple of aisles away. When Lynda began working for Apollo in Dallas she would drive by an account. If the purchasing agent's car wasn't in the lot she wouldn't bother to stop.

Mark was fascinated by machines. A neighbor was horrified to see Mark playing records on our stereo since he was still quite young. When we sold the stereo, a rather large piece of furniture, there were some little bite marks all along one side.

I enrolled him in a nearby preschool. It wasn't a day care center as I had thought. (Mark knew his way to school which was named Pickwickian. "You go down Westpark and turn on St Lo and there's Pickwicky.") I had wanted him to be in day care so he would have playmates, but when I discovered it wasn't the type of school that I had thought, I withdrew him. After that he told everyone who would listen that he was a school dropout—a popular phrase at the time.

Lynda showed promise as a ballerina. Unfortunately her feet wouldn't cooperate. After she went on pointe she had to have toe surgery. Both sides of the toenail on one big toe had to be removed. In spite of her instructor's encouragement to continue, she decided it wasn't worth the pain.

Mark was captured by music when growing up. In fact he still is. He said that his first tape recorder was the best gift he ever received. Even now in noisy restaurants he will comment on the background music being played. Mark and Julie enjoy and collect symphonic albums. Mark has long been an admirer of Cecelia Bartoli and once met her backstage after an operatic performance in Paris. He says she's very nice.

He was active in drama at Humble High School and specialized in duet acting in particular. Mark still stays in contact with many high school friends. They are all married with families and most live in the Dallas area.

There is now an overpass marking the intersection of Kingwood Drive and Highway 59. This had not yet been built when our kids were in school. Mark and his friends still went to Humble High School since Kingwood HS was still under construction. This explains why Mark and three girls were headed to Humble for a play rehearsal. It was dark at the intersection and as they started across, they were T boned by a car heading north.

Since Mark was the only guy in the car he was automatically put in charge. He somehow got everyone to the emergency room and each girl's parents called. It was only then when he was talking to Nick, that he broke down. He was later to say his tape recorder caught fire and he found glass in his underwear. Happily no one in the car sustained any permanent injury. Tana, the driver of the car, and the most seriously injured, even recovered enough to star in the play!

Mark and Jimmy Allen, a neighbor down the street, were friends. They were about twelve at the time. Jimmy big expert that he was, decided it was time Mark learned to drive. His Mom's car was in the driveway with the keys in the ignition. Once in the driver's seat Mark became confused. Which was the accelerator? Which was the brake? This uncertainty led to disaster. He quickly drove the car into the garage, but there was a problem: the garage door was closed. A few minutes later it had fallen off its hinges and rested on the hood of the car. Hysteria reigned! Fortunately Jimmy's father George, was a good friend with a sense of humor. He laughingly related the story to us. The way he described the scene was: both boys were jumping up and down and screaming for help! We paid our part of the damages and the incident was forgotten.

The following happened when Lynda had just started high school. Nick and I announced we needed to run an errand and would return in three or four hours. She intended to go over to her friend Linda Braus' house, but somewhere along the way the plan changed. Instead Linda came to our house. Our other car was in the driveway and Lynda knew where to find the keys.

We returned a couple of hours earlier than planned. "Someone stole the car" was our first reaction. In a few minutes 'our stolen car' rounded the corner with Lyn at the wheel. She was not quite the expert driver she fancied herself to be. As the vehicle came closer the damage became evident. The mirror on the driver's side was hanging uselessly down the side of the car. (This story has an ugly ending that we won't discuss further.)

In all her growing up years Lyn was like having a co-pilot in the car. She was an extra pair of eyes and ears especially when maneuvering through heavy traffic. She also had a real knack for helping me find parking places. It was great to have such a helper, but there was one time I wished she had kept her information to herself. After one outing she had told her father "Mom almost got hit by a cement truck today!" I explained that it was because the visor was down on the passenger's side. Nick said, "can't you come up with something better than that?"

When Lynda was approximately thirteen she and Nick attended the Masters Golf Tournament in Augusta. Morris Hatalsky, a contestant that year, had sent two tickets. Since Lynda was off for spring break and I had already been once, I was glad for her to go with her dad.

The Masters is always at Easter time and it is presumed that the weather will be warm. Lynda and Nick dressed accordingly. When they arrived they were shocked to find the temperature had plummeted. To add to their dilemma the stores had stopped selling winter clothes. Apparently unwilling to miss some sales some stores dug out the heavy clothing and probably did a brisk business. There were no gloves to be found so they wore socks on their hands.

Apparently one of the highlights of the trip was their rent car. Nick recalls it was a beat-up blue car. Augusta must have a lot of pot holes which were filled with water from a recent rain. They enjoyed themselves singing the batman theme song (popular at that time) and yelling "rent car" as Nick deliberately hit every water-filled pot hole he could!

At 3:00am one morning, a loud banging noise woke them. They were on the third floor of the hotel and below them a guy in a white pick-up truck had slid off into the ditch. In his attempt to get back on the road (complicated by an inebriated condition) he was repeatedly banging into the back of a parked car. "I'm going to report that guy!" Nick exclaimed. "No," insisted Lynda, we won't be able to go to the golf course for the next round!" Nick, in spite of her protests, went downstairs to report the damage happening outside the hotel. The police arrived five minutes later and as they were taking Nick's statement, the driver of the pickup walked into the lobby. He was drunk and disheveled. "That's him!" Nick said in surprise. Immediately the police handcuffed him and took him to jail!

Later that morning when court opened, Nick and Lynda identified the man and left in plenty of time to get to the golf course.

This reminded me of something that happened to us several years later. We were returning from a Christmas party across town. We lived in Kingwood. We noticed a car in the next lane repeatedly hitting the rear-end of a vehicle in front of him. Nick decided to steer clear of this guy and sped up. This seemed to attract his attention and he changed lanes and increased his speed in an effort to catch up with us.

We were approaching the Humble exit and decided to get off the freeway as fast as we could. Nick drove straight to the Humble police station a couple of blocks away. We were going in to fill out a report when just then the guy who had been chasing us arrived! He must have spotted our parked car and tried to stop. He was going too fast, hit the curb and the motor died. He was too drunk to realize he had driven into the parking lot of the police station, where an easy arrest was made!

A short time later, a woman who had observed everything that had happened, also arrived. She corroborated our story and added, "I was afraid he was going to run you off the road!"

The dreaded teen-age years and beyond

Mark, an infrequent passenger in the back seat, was reading or sleeping. Lyn and I never depended on him for help. However this trait was to help him in the future for all the traveling he would do. Mark had the remarkable ability to sleep in cars, planes and trains. It mattered not. He would arrive fresh as the proverbial daisy while the rest of us were frazzled and bleary-eyed.

When we flew to Paris to visit Mark we were booked on an overnight flight. Neither Nick nor I would have been considered seasoned overseas travelers. Nevertheless Nick had it all figured out. His "well-thought out plan" was if he played eighteen holes of golf and drank a glass of wine prior to take-off surely he would sleep all the way. As a result of this clever strategy, he stayed awake all night and arrived exhausted.

Later he was to learn that alcohol at 37,000 feet is not a sedative! With jet lag on top of that we were ready to crash at our hotel. Mark had other ideas and had been waiting eagerly to show us the sights of Paris. We couldn't disappoint our son, so off we went. At one point Nick groaned, "I can't feel my feet anymore!" Upon hearing that, Mark took pity on us and we got a day off. As a result, we enjoyed Notre Dame Cathedral much more the next day.

Years later Lynda had by this time sharpened her driving skills and had a license. Nick had promised to buy her a car. As she drove the Toyota Corolla off the lot she asked "Dad, don't you think it looks like a Mercedes?"

The dreaded high school years arrived (dreaded by us not by them.) Mark, at Humble High School was selected as the "outstanding student in French" for his class. He discovered he had an aptitude for language and studied French and Russian at Baylor University. We asked both kids to attend Baylor for their first two years. If they didn't like it they could transfer with our blessings. We had three reasons for this: 1. It was close to home 2. It was close to home and 3. It was close to home. Actually, being Baptist, we hoped Baylor would have a moral and spiritual influence in our children's lives. In retrospect this was probably wishful thinking. They agreed to attend Baylor and in the end that's where they got their degrees.

Lyn won the title "Miss Teen of Texas" in her junior year of high school. In her senior year she was colonel of the drill team and voted "best combination of Beauty and Brains." Following graduation from BU, she moved to Dallas and went to work in her father's business as a salesperson.

LYNDA AND FRIEND MELANIE

Mark, on the other hand, chose adventure abroad. He spent over a couple of years in Paris studying at the Sorbonne. From there he lived in Toronto, Chicago and ended up in New York. He loved New York most. We visited him in Paris, Chicago and New York, but never quite made it to Toronto. In all these locations, he worked for Berlitz as a translator. Finally, just like Dorothy, he decided "there's no place like home!" Well, Texas anyway. He too, returned to Dallas and worked for Nick.

MARK GETS ACQUAINTED
WITH HIS NIECE AND NEPHEW

In between all these places Nick and Mark took a vacation together, in fact two. Nick recalls with pleasure the time he and Mark spent in Seattle. My always-be-on-your-guard-because-who-knows-what-might-happen husband remembers the park where he and Mark *actually* took a nap! I wish someone had photographed that. In fact it was so extraordinary he mentions it any time "Seattle" comes up in a conversation. In the spring of 2000 they also vacationed in New Orleans, compliments of Mark, to visit the War Memorial Museum. They are making plans to go there again.

Mark has the uncanny ability to remember the exact year and sometimes the day and month of something that happened in the past. When we can't recall a date which is quite often we say in unison, "let's ask Mark!"

Lynda and I spent a long weekend in Galveston. It was a wonderful time and we enjoyed being away from home and by ourselves. When we prepared to leave, we discovered someone had broken the side window on the car—this occurred just outside the Commodore Hotel on the seawall. They were apparently attempting to steal the car. I was distressed at the damage but Lynda said, "don't let it ruin the time that we had!" I was so proud of her. That was what I was supposed to say to her—and instead she said it to me!

CHAPTER 7

MEANWHILE, WHAT WAS HAPPENING IN BIG "D"

The Dallas division of Apollo was a heavy load in the years between 1971 and 1988. It kept Joe and Nick going back and forth to Dallas every other week—sometimes for a few days and other times for an entire week. At the heart of the problem was a string of bad management hires.

Dean the first manager came highly recommended, but was not the man for the job. He had worked for a large corporation and was great at carrying out orders but not giving them. Ollie succeeded Dean. While he was a good salesman he did not have management experience. Tom Wilms followed Dean and Ollie and next came Chuck. His "sins" were listed at length in chapter 5. Following Chuck was Roy who assumed so much authority that he would say "no" even before the question was asked. At long last, Walt arrived and continued in that capacity until Nick sold the company.

Dean was right about one thing, rather one person. Betty Shelton recently divorced with two young children worked for a local paper house in Dallas. She had worked there for 19 years. Betty was employed as a part-time sales person and part-time secretary, but wanted a full-time selling job. Dean knew her good reputation in the industry and hired her. She was to become the first woman salesperson in the Southwest at that time.

Betty would be the "rock" the glue that kept Dallas going in the months and years ahead. She was not only very attractive, but dressed to the nines. She knew her products and formed loyal friendships easily. Betty would have been on anybody's short list of desirable employees.

NICK AND BETTY

The very day she reported for work Dean had just been fired. Betty cried! Nick took her hand and reassured her that everything was going to be okay. He vividly recalled the first sales call he made with her. The company was Bennett Printing. The buyer for the company had placed orders with Betty over the phone for years. She introduced herself and Nick and the buyer exclaimed, "oh my God,

Miss Betty!" After that first call Nick knew Betty would be a resounding success. "She was a natural!"

Following Betty several other talented salespeople were added. Among these were John and David. The sales volume grew and Dallas was looking good! On the negative side, weak management remained a problem. Roy's dismissal created a temporary vacancy at that position.

On New Year's Day 1988 Nick received a phone call that changed everything. Once more Dallas was plunged into chaos. John was the caller and told Nick that with great regret he had concluded he must leave Apollo. Butler a large, established paper company was starting a packaging division. They had made him an attractive offer he felt he must accept.

Nick's belief was that in addition to Betty's, John's sales were essential to the success of the Dallas division. John had excellent work habits and his many customers were very loyal to him. If John left it could mean a complete loss of the Dallas operation. All the weeks, months and years Nick and Joe invested in the enterprise were endangered.

Nick was stunned. He had no idea John was contemplating such a drastic career move. As far as he knew he and John had a good relationship. They talked and Nick asked him to reconsider and that he (Nick) would call him back. When he did, His wife said he was inaccessible and the next day John started work at Butler.

After the shock of John's call, Nick said, "I know the Bible says all things work together for good to those who love God and are called according to His purpose, but right now I just can't see it!" It was the lowest time of his life up to that point. We prayed. As I was reading the Bible the next day the Lord impressed on my heart this scripture:

Isaiah 41:10-13 "Fear not, for I am with you; be not dismayed, for I am your God. I will uphold you with My righteous right hand. V11 Behold, all those who were incensed against you shall be ashamed and disgraced; they shall be as nothing, and those who strive with you shall perish. V12 You shall seek them and not find them—those who contended with you shall be as nothing, as a nonexistent thing. V13 For I, the Lord your God, will hold your right hand, saying to you fear not, I will help you."

Years prior to this Ken Forsch a pitcher for the Astros baseball team read the verse "for I, the Lord . . . will hold your right hand" and believed God. In his following turn on the mound he pitched a no hitter! This account was printed in the Houston Post. It's a powerful verse.

Nick was "struck down but not destroyed" and soon the old fighting spirit began to resurface. Although it appeared to be a David vs Goliath fight, Nick took two of his employees and headed to Dallas.

One of the employees was Walt Chandler, a staunch Christian. He offered to move to Dallas if that was needed. Nick and Walt were close friends because they had the same optimistic business outlook. Walt would come in daily after work and have a cigarette with Nick. He would inevitably say, "do you want to hear something good?"

Before the group could even reach Dallas they received word Troy had resigned to work for Butler. Troy was the purchasing agent. Who would be the next to leave was the question on everyone's mind.

After Nick's arrival he hastily called a meeting and discovered the full extent of the treachery. There had been no "enticing offer from Butler." John had been carefully planning this for months. He had lied to all his accounts telling them Apollo was on the verge of bankruptcy. He said he had discovered this "fact" and felt impelled to leave to protect both himself and them! He asked each account to buy from him for at least a year or he wouldn't be able to leave. They apparently agreed.

Nick's next act was to fire David, John's brother-in-law who planned to stay behind as a source of information for John. He was promptly awarded a job at Butler.

Following all this negative news Nick received a pleasant surprise. John's co-workers were elated he had left. He apparently was affable and friendly only to those who could help him (which of course included Nick.) But to anyone who was not of particular use he would often be rude or indifferent.

The other employees had decided that Apollo was a good place to work. No one else left even though several had been approached by Butler. Walt Chandler did move to Dallas and as earlier stated, remained as manager. At long last this gave the division the stability it lacked.

About the time all this drama was unfolding our daughter, Lynda joined the company. She already lived in Dallas after graduation. She had a low paying few responsibilities job and was looking for a greater challenge. The Lord sent us Lynda in our greatest hour of need. All the words that described Betty also applied to our Lynda. Betty never fearing competition quickly befriended Lynda.

Although several were to follow in her footsteps, Lynda was the first company employee to reach the two million dollar mark in sales in one year. The buttons nearly popped off Nick's shirt he was so proud! A few years later her future husband Tony, would sell three million dollars in one year. Are we proud of our family or what?

One further word about Butler Paper Co and John. Although John was the instigator, Butler agreed to hire as many of Apollo's people as they could. Over time this would leave the company no choice but to declare bankruptcy. When John left Butler also encouraged him to take a list of Betty's accounts. Nick arranged for the sheriff, under a "TRO" (temporary restraining order), to retrieve the list. It was discovered in John's desk drawer. Amazing! Butler was sold three time since then. Their memory has been totally erased.

Nick and I (after a struggle) have forgiven John. He's a very conscientious worker and the word is that he has done well and prospered. Romans 12:19 "Beloved, do not avenge yourselves . . . for it is written vengeance is mine, I will repay" says the Lord.

After this major disruption things became more routine with Walt at the helm. He faithfully called Nick whenever he faced an unfamiliar or daunting situation. Nick, of course, was happy to give constructive advice.

Walt and his wife Dana had adopted a baby boy while they lived in Houston. Nick had been instrumental in assisting in this process. Ford was their pride and joy but died at an early age. They often expressed thankfulness for the time they spent with him and for their subsequent daughter-in-law and grandchild.

Greg Raindl a close friend to Walt was instrumental in Walt's success. Besides Betty, Lynda and Tony, already mentioned, many other employees spent years helping build the Dallas division. To name a few: Alan Lavender, Brenda Watley, Cathy Speier, Lorraine LaDoux, Bob McDonald, Bob Goodman and Brad Crawford. This group formed the backbone of the sales force. Inside Neil Burns, Beverly Kitchen, Bree Brownlow and Gary Shook assisted Walt by helping provide support. Who could forget Melvin Price a mainstay in the warehouse? Just as in Houston many additional employees were to follow.

Neil Burns deserves special mention. Neil started working in the warehouse at Apollo Houston. He offered to move to Dallas to fulfill a particular need Nick had at the time. From there he rose to warehouse manager and purchasing agent. Neil is a special person.

To our delight Mark as stated in the previous chapter came home to Texas. He settled in Dallas as his permanent home. When he first came he didn't intended to stay long. He thought of Dallas merely as a place he did not want to live. How ironic that he barring unforeseen circumstances, will probably live there for the rest of his life. God often overrules our plans!

MARK AND LYNDA REUNITED IN DALLAS

Mark bought a house and began working at Apollo. He found his niche as the "I.T. "person. As far back as anyone can remember Mark was preaching to Nick that the company needed a website! It was a hard sell since his father to this day, hates computers. Fortunately others in the company recognized the wisdom of this—and

Mark got his website established. He published the first company newsletter and called it "paper clips."

Mark was right of course. He as well as others could see how vital a website was to the growth of the company. Nick sees progress as beneficial but also with a downside. Examples: because of Velcro children no longer can tie their shoes. They haven't learned to tell time without a digital clock. Store clerks can't make change unless prompted by a machine. People are required to think less. The intention is good but the results are mixed.

Nick tells of the time he was buying tile for a project at home. The man sat at his computer complaining about the slowness of the program. Nick asked, with some degree of sarcasm, "why don't you get up from your chair and walk a few feet to the warehouse and check the number of tile for yourself?" Nick feels that computers often take the place of common sense and encourage laziness.

Love is in the air

Mark's grandmother (and it goes without saying, his whole family) was relieved when Mark came home from Paris. Even though New York could not be considered close, he was at least on this side of the Atlantic. When he returned to Texas we were all ecstatic.

Several years later at the age of 38 Mark met Julie. Mark's Aunt Ann predicted: whatever else she is, Mark's wife *will* be intelligent! He got the complete package.

Julie was not only smart but beautiful and talented as well. (The girl even has a great family!)

The day before Mark's wedding we hired a limo to take us to Dallas. There were four of us: Nick, Nanny, Ann and me. It was such a special day for Nick's mom. She was so happy and excited that Mark was getting married! We couldn't think of anything else to give her that she didn't already have.

We stopped at a small town on the way to Dallas. I bought coffee for the group. The girl behind the counter asked if we were "anybody." She was obviously disappointed that George and Barbara Bush were not with us—and that we were basically "nobodies."

Following their wedding Mark and Julie settled in Mark's house. It was adequate for them but they knew that when an additional arrival came, they would be seriously overcrowded. They searched and found a larger place that fit their needs.

Although Julie was several years younger than Mark, time was still a factor. Soon after they decided to try the fertility drug route. Before long four little bodies were fighting for space in Julie's womb. Baby D died early in the pregnancy. Little Lucy succumbed a couple of days before her brother Will and sister Annie. All were lost for reasons known only to our Lord. We are certain that In the future when Mark and Julie are united with them in heaven, the little ones will already be aware of how dearly their parents loved them and fought to save them.

Approximately a year later they learned of a baby that had been born to a single mom. She desired to keep him but had limited help and little education. She had arrived at the painful decision that it would be best to allow him to be adopted. Mark and Julie learned of her plight and made the process as easy for her as they could. She was comforted to know her baby would be in a loving Christian home. By then he was three months old. Mark and Julie named him Zachary John. Zachary means "God remembers." Next biological son, Luke Davis Nicholson burst on the scene on November 28th of the following year.

After the deaths of the triplets and prior to Zachary's adoption, Mark and Julie were instrumental in starting a "Grief Share" ministry. Through it they have reached out to many hurting people in a variety of situations. They are passing on to others comfort they themselves have received.

Mark needed to find fulltime employment. He resigned from Apollo when Nick sold the company and was working as a freelance translator, but became somewhat inactive during the time they lost the triplets. During this time Mark worked as a volunteer at Watermark. Since they knew of his interest and his aptitude for audio work, he was tapped to join the staff. (He also needed his family to be covered by insurance.) Watermark was the church where they were already members and where they had established their Grief Share ministry.

Just as with the three older grandchildren, (more about them later in the chapter) it has been such a wonderful experience to see the two younger grandchildren grow and change. Zachary is sweet and laid back. Luke is intense and "wired."

THE BEAUTIFUL NICHOLSONS:
MARK, LUKE, JULIE AND ZACHARY

Zachary loves dolphins, cars, trucks, airplanes and—butterflies! He will never be in danger of having ADD. I have observed the child play with one vehicle for hours on end. His concentration is unusual for one so young. He is three and a half and he has possessed this quality for at least a year now! Remarkable.

A few "Z" stories. One day Mark was taking Zachary to the pediatrician. By his own admission he was driving rather fast and passing slower-moving traffic. Zachary from his vantage point in the back seat observed, "Daddy is winning!"

One day we were loading up to go to the mall. Zachary was already in his chair. He watched as I struggled to climb into the van. "I will help you, Maamo!" he exclaimed as he grabbed my sweater and pulled me up into the seat. Julie recognized a teaching moment and complimented him for being a "gentleman who helps ladies."

The last time we visited in Dallas, Zachary had switched his interest to dolphins. I remarked about the cute little flippers on their sides— like wings. "In fact there's one near the top of his head as well!" "Oh, no, Maamo, that one on the top is a dorsal fin!" (I hope we can still converse by the time he's in first grade.)

There was a very elaborate train display in Dallas. Zachary was entranced! It was located in a shopping mall and he was taken to see it numerous times. One would think that after a while it would lose some of its charm. This was not the case and each time when it was time to leave, he was reluctant to go. Loudly reluctant!

After I write this I promise to stop apologizing for this children's DVD. I bought and sent to the boys a DVD with the song "the wheels on the bus." The part I regretted at the time was the second song: "dem bones." Somehow it didn't seem appropriate to send a song picturing dancing skeletons to boys of two and three years old. Surprisingly the boys loved both the song and the video. Mark and Julie turned it into a positive by purchasing interlocking skeletal pieces painted in white on gray foam. These can be put together like a puzzle. This has helped the boys learn the parts of the human body.

(They are also well versed in naming the planets of our solar system.)

WHAT AN AMAZING PICTURE, THEY ARE SO STILL!

While Zachary is enamored by cars Luke loves animals. Zachary is rather stand-offish and frightened of them, but not Luke! The more of them the better. My favorite Luke story: one evening Mark and Julie had a baby sitter for the boys. She was having them help her with simple chores. Z seemed to be fine with the program but Luke protested, "I'm too young to work!" Luke is our entertainer and is prone to dance even when no music is playing. His singing repertoire includes but is not necessarily limited to: "Jesus loves me" and "Frosty the Snowman." What fun to be a part of their growing up years!

Even before Mark found Julie, Lynda and Tony discovered each other. One of Lynda's customers was Patterson Dental. A really cute guy was the buyer there—but he was a tough sell! Lynda had to cut prices, take inventory and promise good service before he would buy from Apollo. He was just getting her attention. (In much the same way Nick got mine years ago!) Once they met, a serious relationship started.

Tony Snider was transferred to Austin for a few months and they both regarded this as a test. They decided if they still felt the same way after being apart during this time, they would marry. Fifteen years and three children later it seems a safe bet the relationship is going to last.

Tony as already mentioned, came to work at Apollo, Dallas. He is personally very handsome with a personality to match. One of Tony's main assets is that he has a "sense of fun" that's contagious. It's as though he is hugely enjoying himself and inviting you to join him. From years of lifting weights Tony is *very* strong! Lynda shops for him and finds it hard to get shirts big enough in the arms! (No complaints. Most of us have trouble buying something that's big enough in the *waist!*)

Besides doing three million dollars in sales, Tony was able to successfully complete an MBA degree from SMU. This was no doubt helpful in later starting his own business in Charlotte, NC. (Did I mention the boy is smart?)

ANN, LYNDA AND NANNY
WITH FIRST GRANDCHILD, LAURA

On November 8, 1997 Laura arrived. Our first grandchild spent her early childhood in Dallas. One of my earliest recollections was in Tony and Lynda's apartment. They lived there while their house in Flower Mound was being finished. There were two couches stored side by side in the living room. Laura laughing with delight would literally run across the first couch and throw herself on the second one. All the while I was lecturing her with as much conviction as I could, "couches are to sit on, Laura, not walk on!" No one could get upset with Laura she was such a loveable little scamp!

While Laura was still in the womb Tony would talk to her and she learned to recognize his voice. After her delivery she was crying, but when she heard his voice she seemed comforted and immediately stopped.

Veggie Tales were first marketed when Laura was in pre-school. I read to her the story of Madame Blueberry. Madame Blueberry's house fell out of the tree and broke apart! Laura was so heartbroken she flung herself across the bed and sobbed uncontrollably. Madame Blueberry will never know what a sympathetic listener she had that day. I tried in vain to tell her the story had a happy ending. (I'm not sure we ever finished that story.)

One day Lynda and I took Laura to the Fort Worth zoo. Laura fell in love with all the animals but her favorite was a white Siberian tiger. It was glassed in and the temperature controlled. Laura pressed her little hands and face against the glass and said, "I want to pet him!"

As Laura started school Lynda began to dread phone calls. She started getting almost daily calls from Laura's teacher saying she had hit some unsuspecting child that day. Finally after this had gone on for awhile, Tony sat Laura down and told her he would be waiting outside the school. If her teacher called and told him she had hit someone, he would come in, get her and give her a spanking.

Magically the situation seemed to correct itself overnight. Lynda never received another phone call from the teacher. Since that time Laura has made friends easily, enjoyed her teachers each year and made excellent grades.

Laura came to visit us for the first time in our present house. She was still quite young and the house was big and scary to her. She followed me everywhere holding on to the bottom of my robe. I looked like a queen with my little page behind me carrying my train.

The last time Nick and I were in Charlotte we went to a volleyball game in which Laura was playing. We also attended Blake's soccer game and Katy's praise dance performance. Of course all three were outstanding!

Laura is so very special. I know God has wonderful work planned for her.

HERE THEY ARE BEFORE THEY GOT BIG:
LAURA, KATY AND BLAKE

Blake came along two years after Laura. He, like Laura, is very unique. He loves sports and like his dad, enjoys tests of strength. On one of our visit, he demonstrated five one arm push-ups in rapid succession! He's also an avid reader and an electronic game enthusiast. He surprised me one day by very expertly fixing something on our digital camera and explaining its various functions. He also can operate the home theater. This is complicated enough that his mother has no interest in investing the necessary time to learn how to do it.

All three Snider children love their younger cousins. Somehow it seems more natural for girls. We have these built-in nurturing instincts. One weekend Mark and Zachary flew to Charlotte for a visit. We were there too. Zachary was of course adored by all, but I was surprised to see the enjoyment Blake had when he and Zachary were playing by themselves in the hot tub. Blake gave Z his undivided attention and Zachary was delighted to have such a "big boy" pay attention to him. Blake is exceptionally tendered hearted.

It's my delight to pray with Blake each night while I'm there (in fact with all three)—and to rub his back! He's such a sweetheart. May the Lord use each one of his unique gifts in the future.

Prior to Katy's last birthday I had purchased a birthday card for her and asked Nick to write a birthday greeting on it. I, of course, was talking about our granddaughter, Katy Snider, aged 10. Nick asked, "Is Katie ninety three now?" "What are you talking about?" He repeated the question. I finally realized we were on different subjects. (After fifty years together this doesn't happen often.) <u>He</u> was talking about our friend, Katie Watson.

The first story that comes to mind about Katy was the time we asked her what was going to happen after she finished sixth grade. She said "well, I guess you go to college!"

Lynda related this story. One morning last year she was preparing breakfast. Having just bought a new school blouse for Laura, she commented that she looked very nice in it. Blake, who is not always at his best in the early morning (I can sympathize, Blake) said grumpily, "no one told me I look nice this morning!" Lynda gave him a look that said, "don't start that with me, Blake!" Katy saw it and quickly said, "you sure look pretty this morning, Mom!" Of course Lynda had to laugh at Katy's obvious attempt to keep the peace. "She's our diplomat," Lynda was to say.

Katy the one who cheerfully runs errands, is quick with compliments and always in a cheerful mood. Like her two older siblings she is athletic. She has found her niche in praise dance. Lynda and Tony are blessed with three children that love the Lord and are scholarly athletes.

OUR SECOND GORGEOUS FAMILY,
LAURA, TONY, KATY, LYNDA AND BLAKE SNIDER

CHAPTER 8 ✏

NICK, DID YOU <u>REALLY</u> DO THAT?

The following stories about Nick are revealing. We view life very differently at times. He has a tendency to do and say things that have made me nervous over the years. Overall I would have to admit the things he has said and done have produced good results.

*   *   *

Nick operates on the assumption that everyone enjoys a good laugh to lighten the hum drum of "business as usual." One day last year as we were checking out at a local store, the female employee requested routine information about our account. She asked Nick, "what is your telephone number?" He replied with mock indignation, "what do you mean asking me for my telephone number in front of my wife?"

*   *   *

Shopping with Nick is an adventure. In our early craft days we would enter the store and purchase the products we needed. In the process Nick would end up talking to the buyer or owner. Ever the salesman he would end up selling them paper supplies and making a whole lot more money from them than what we had spent. At times I was called upon to do detective work. He would often request, "bring me a sample of the paper towels they use in the ladies' room."

* * *

In a store in Old Town Spring one shop owner got a real shock. As Nick and I were leaving some shoppers were coming in. He announced loudly, "I own this store and everything is half-price today! Come right in ladies and load up!" The shop owner standing nearby didn't know whether to laugh or cry. The best she could do was exclaim vehemently, "he's not the owner! Everything is exactly as marked!" I was glad we were leaving that chaos!

Nick had an ophthalmologist appointment. It was in the early days of Apollo. Patience has never been one of Nick's strong virtues and he was especially impatient that day because of a heavy work load at the office.

He sat patiently, for him, the first hour. As he watched patient after patient go in to see the doctor ahead of him he became irritated. Finally he left after telling the receptionist he would call later. As he left the parking garage and discovered he was required to pay $1.00 something snapped.

When he reached his office he called and asked to speak to the doctor. He got the standard answer, "he's with a patient." "I'll wait!" At last the doctor came on the line. Nick expressed his displeasure and ended by saying, "I want you to send me $1.00 to pay for parking!" Again he received the standard reply, "sir I regret your inconvenience but I can't do that." Nick said anger rising in his voice, "you don't know me and I don't know you. I do where your designated parking space is in the garage. Some night I'll be waiting for you and give you such a beating your mother won't recognize you!"

Shortly afterwards, I received an envelope from a doctor's office with a $1.00 inside. I called Nick and told him about the $1.00. Then he had to confess what had happened. In his defense Nick has mellowed considerably in these intervening years.

* * *

Nick and I were newlyweds when this situation took place. I was still working for Braniff Airways. These meetings were held in the evenings. Since this was supposed to be company business, spouses were not included. Our station manager, Homer had a tendency to drink a little too much on these occasions. After two or three drinks he would approach a female employee and make some "suggestions." These to my knowledge, seldom if ever were carried through. Homer was considered quite harmless and more or less a joke.

During one such meeting it seemed to be my turn. Homer made some vague "hints" which I immediately brushed off. "Well what did Homer have to say to you last night?" someone laughingly asked the next day. The situation was so humorous I decided to share the joke with Nick. If I had known my husband better I would not have said a word about the encounter. Too late!

The next day Nick called Homer and expressed outrage that he would say such things to me. He offered to meet Homer in the airport lobby after work. Homer declined. A wise decision. It's best to leave irate husbands, fresh out of the Marine Corps alone!

Braniff Airways was abuzz with this latest juicy bit of gossip. Homer contacted me and I lied convincingly. "I certainly hope you don't think *I* told him!" Homer wasn't eager to pursue the matter further, so that seemed to end it. Perhaps it actually helped him. Hopefully he realized he either shouldn't drink so much, or failing that keep his mouth shut. I left Braniff soon after that so I have no way of knowing. Homer was undoubtedly glad to be rid of both of us Nicholsons!

*   *   *

The following story takes place in the Dallas office. The warehouse manager, Jerry was on Nick's "bad" list. Jerry had accumulated a pile of unreturned merchandise that grew larger with each passing week. "I'll get on it just as soon as I return from vacation," he promised just as he had many times before. In addition to the stack of stuff, the warehouse had become an absolute disaster. It had become impossible to work there effectively.

When Jerry left on vacation Nick called Charles Roche to come to Dallas for a special project. Charles had experience in laying out warehouses and the time had come for a complete overhaul. Not only would the costly merchandise be returned, but the warehouse would be revamped as well.

When Charles arrived they both realized what a daunting task they faced. The work had to be completed in one week—before Jerry's return. Charles had to change all the rack locations, then Nick operating the tow motor had to move all the inventory to the designated space.

They contacted a labor force in Dallas. The company sent out a very large, strong black man. By a happy coincidence he, Charles and Nick were all former Marines. His name was Chris and before long the trio was bonding. Although the work was hard and long hours were required, they were having fun. Harkening back to their marine days, Nick pretended to be the D.I. "Not there private, over there!" Nick was later to say he was intentionally swatting Chris rather hard with his "swagger stick" (broom handle.) Although it's hard for women to understand this type of roughhousing, they were having a wonderful time.

As the week drew to a close, they were all three dead tired. Nick and Charles had to drive back to Houston and resume the work they had left behind. In spite of this they were all three sorry to see the week end. Nick was so pleased with Chris' work that he asked his address and telephone number. He promised the next time an opening occurred, they would call him.

They continued to work through Sunday and Jerry returned to work the following day. Nick and Charles were there to greet him. Jerry quickly discovered he would not be there to enjoy the newly revamped warehouse; that he was fired. Because he had been with the company so long, he couldn't believe he was now unemployed!

Nick replied that he didn't fire him, he had fired himself by his job performance, actually the lack of it.

I wish this was the end of the story. When Nick and Charles returned to Houston they were sent a copy of the Dallas Morning News the following week. There on the front page was a picture of their friend Chris. He believed his girlfriend was seeing other men. Knowing she was hospitalized, he brazenly entered her room and slit her throat. We have no further information on Chris. We can only hope he is somewhere under close supervision!

*   *   *

Nick and I have different mindsets regarding money; specifically the spending and saving of money.

A friend had a particular accessory in her house that we admired. She said she had found it in a certain River Oaks store and recommended we shop there the next time we were in that area. A couple of weeks later we were running errands in that part of town.

For those not acquainted with Houston, River Oaks is a very upscale shopping center. Just the thought of entering the designated store was intimidating. As predicted I found an amazing vase, perfect for the place I needed to accessorize. Not only was the vase amazing—so was the price tag.

"I wonder if I can get them to discount it" Nick wondered aloud. At first I couldn't speak. When I found my voice I said, "are you <u>actually</u> going to ask them to lower the price? This isn't a flea market—the price is the price!" "Wait here, he commanded. I didn't wait there, I went to another part of the store as far away as possible.

A few minutes later he returned triumphantly and announced they had significantly lowered the price. I have no information to pass on to you as to how he does this. I think it has to do with some magic incantation. He seems able to do it over and over regardless of the circumstances. One thing I know for sure—I can't.

*   *   *

Nick does have at least one Achille's heel. His sense of direction is deplorable. In fact we are both directionally challenged. In the past we would decide which way we thought was correct and then go the opposite way. It worked for us every time. Fortunately we now have a GPS, a present from Mark and Julie.

One time in Dallas as Nick was making calls with Lynda, they were fortunate to have Neil Burns chauffer them around. He had transferred from Houston, at Nick's request to run the Dallas warehouse. By this time Neil knew the city well.

In early 1988 Nick found it necessary to go to Dallas by car. He was accompanied by two employees, Walt Chandler and Jerry Maness. When they arrived at the city limits they asked Nick the way to his office. Nick had no idea. To further complicate matters they were arriving on the weekend and the office was closed. (At this point neither Neil nor Lynda had jobs in Dallas yet!)

In the past Dallas sales people had picked him up at the airport. From there they made sales calls and then return him either to the office or his hotel. The next morning they would repeat the process again. To this day Nick doesn't know his way around Dallas.

Finally by consulting a Dallas business card, they discovered his office was somewhere on Valley View in Farmers' Branch. After asking two or three people they arrived at their destination. They had a good laugh at the expense of "Mr. Always Prepared."

* * *

One of Apollo's accounts was a company called Johnson Supply. The purchasing agent's name was Ruby. Nick and one of his salesmen were out making calls in the area so decided to call on the company. A phone call revealed that Ruby was in the hospital recovering from an appendectomy. Since the hospital was located close by they decided to pay a visit.

Ruby was glad to see them and they talked for awhile. All of a sudden, Nick announced he wanted to see her incision. He walked over to the bed and lifted one corner of the spread. She was taken by surprise and indignantly said, "Nick, don't you dare! You stop that right now!" All the while she hugged the covers tightly around her. As the two men doubled over with laughter, It quickly dawned on her that her modesty was not in danger. At that point she heartily joined in.

* * *

Edgar Allen Poe named after the famous writer, was a small shriveled-up man with a personality to match. He worked for a company called Southwest Galvanizing. Roland Rollins called on him faithfully but had never received an order. Mr. Poe continually promised to "give him the business" but for whatever reason it never happened.

Roland reported to Nick what "a mean old man" he was. Southwest Galvanizing was a large company and mean old man or not, he represented lots of dollars in sales. Roland asked Nick to go with him to call on Mr. Poe. Nick agreed.

When they entered his office he was down on his knees behind his desk going through file folders. Nick's opening greeting was, "you mean old SOB whatever you're doing down there you should be praying!" "You're kinda spunky—what do you want?" demanded Mr. Poe. Nick shot back that he wanted an order. "You have been telling Roland you're going to give him the business. You've been giving him "the business" all right—now we want an order! "Who are you?" Mr. Poe inquired irritably. "Do you have a business card?" Nick presented his card and Mr. Poe promptly turned and threw it in the wastebasket. Nick calmly walked around the desk and retrieved it from the trash. After this exchange Mr. Poe began giving Roland orders and they continued until Mr. Poe left the company.

Upon learning that he had retired, Nick called him to thank him for all the business he had given Apollo over the years. Salty as ever when he took the call he asked, "what do you want?" Nick told him and he immediately softened. After they had conversed for a time, Mr. Poe said "we have had some fun haven't we?"

* * *

One day when Nick was at the Dallas office Ron Edwards asked him if he would make a call with him on the Libby Glass Co. in McKinney, Texas.

Ron routinely would take their inventory and call in the order to Apollo's office. The following day it would be automatically delivered.

Nick and Ron called on Leta, the Libby Glass purchasing agent. As they were leaving Nick asked if there was anything Apollo could do better. Leta thought for a minute and answered, "No." But a moment later she said, "yes there is one thing." Nick thought to himself, "oh no, I may have opened a can of worms. Why did I have to ask that?"

Leta complained, "Libby Glass is a large company. By the time I have sent the purchase order to be typed and sent down to 'receiving' the merchandise is already there."

Nick laughed. "I can't believe we've created problems by delivering orders too fast. That's a first!" Then he instructed Ron not to call it in until a day later. "That'll work," nodded Leta.

* * *

Nick enjoyed making calls on Houston Foam Plastics. He knew everyone there and Patty Harrington was a special friend. This time they had hired a new receptionist. He decided to play a joke on his friend Patty. When the new girl asked if she could help him he said, "I'd like to see Sister Patty." "Who?" she inquired. He repeated the request. "What is your name?" "Tell her I'm the 'Reverend' from the Church of What's Happening Now. I'm here to pick up the $100.00 donation she promised to give me."

She left to go back to Patty's office and was gone for some time. When she returned she told Nick, "she'll be right out." The door to the reception office opened a crack and Patty peeked around the door.

When she saw Nick she exclaimed, "damn you, Nick!" Both of them cracked up laughing. She concluded, "you scared me to death!" To this day (thirty years later) she's still "Sister Patty" and he is the "Reverend!"

* * *

Nick and I were at Lowe's Anatole Hotel in Dallas on a Saturday. He had been up there during the week and we had stayed in Dallas overnight. We enjoyed having lunch at Lowe's. We saw the gift store was open and as we approached, we noticed two obviously hand-painted ceramic urns on pedestals. We were looking for something to decorate our new atrium. Nick priced them. They were $240.00 each. That seemed reasonable. "If you like the shape of them you could repaint them to match something," he remarked.

We looked at the price tag more closely. The price was $24,000.00 not $240.00 as we had first thought. Forewarned regarding gift store prices we went in anyway.

The store clerk was a very distinguished-looking gray haired lady. She showed us several items she thought we might like. We were assured that if we *really* liked the painted ceramic urns, the artist himself was arriving the very next week. He would be delighted to "sign" them for us! We thanked her but said we were from Houston and couldn't make it back the following week—although we would have *loved* to have met the artist since we had admired his work so much.

As we continued to chat about other items we couldn't afford, she mentioned her husband had built the hotel. The poor lady no doubt had delusions of grandeur. Here she was working in a gift shop on Saturday and trying to make herself feel important.

Meanwhile, Nick always in pursuit of an order for paper products noticed they needed bubble wrap to ship their expensive gift items. He mentioned he had a company there in Dallas. He asked for her business card and promised to have a salesman call. As we left she cautioned, "this is my private line. Please don't give this number to anyone but your salesman. We thanked her and remarked how pleasant it had been to talk with her.

Outside the shop Nick read the name on the card: Mrs. Trammel Crow. I kept up a steady conversation about all the decorative items we had seen in the store.

When Nick finally spoke he said, with a far-away look and a note of wonder in his voice, "I have Mrs. Trammel Crow's private telephone number!"

E P I L O G U E

M. E. "NICK" NICHOLSON
President/CEO

14345 Northwest Frwy.
Houston, TX 77040
(713) 329-5678
FAX (713) 329-5656
www.apollopaper.com

4151 State Hwy. 121
Grapevine, TX 76051
M (972) 724-2828
FAX (972) 724-2808

1816 Finfeather
Bryan, TX 77803
(877) 329-2345
FAX (877) 329-5657

DENVER HARBOR BOY JOINS MARINES

Morris Nicholson, son of Mr. and Mrs. J. J. Nicholson, 207 Woolworth left April 25 for boot camp, San Diego, California after enlisting into the Marine Corps for two years. Morris graduated for Stephen F. Austin high school in 1954.

FOND MEMORIES OF THE RED BIRDS IN JUNIOR HIGH DAYS

Redbirds Beat Cardinals, 6-5

The Redbirds of the Denver Harbor Little League beat the Cardinals of the National Little League, 6-5, Tuesday night at Denver Harbor Park. Morris Nicholson went the distance for the Redbirds to get the win and struck out 14.

Wilson was the powerhouse for the Cardinals. In three times at the plate he hit two home runs and a single and batted in four runs. Donald Roberts had a home run in the first inning with two on for the winners.

Cardinals   501 002—5 4 9
Redbirds   300 390—6 6 9
  Baglse, McLain (7) Ashmore (4) and Wilson; Nicholson and Roberts.

Red Birds Annex Denver Harbor Title

Morris Nicholson bested Kenneth Stevens in a pitchers' duel Saturday night at the Denver Harbor Field as the Red Birds eked out a 1-0 win over the Eagles for the championship of the Denver Harbor Little League. Each pitcher allowed one hit.

The winning run came in the sixth frame when Nicholson walked and came in on a double by Kenneth Williams. Nicholson struck out 16 and Stevens 13.

CREATIVE COSMETIC PHOTOGRAPHY CIRCA
1956-BOOT CAMP YEARBOOK. NICK'S LEFT FRONT
TOOTH WAS NON-SURGICALLY REMOVED COURTESY
OF SOLTYCIAK. HIS GRAVE INFRACTION: SAYING "I"
INSTEAD OF "PRIVATE NICHOLSON." (THERE ARE NO
PRIVATE I'S IN THE MARINE CORPS)

COMPILED AND PRESENTED BY DAN E. PICINI, CEO OF DURATEST CORPORATION OF NEW JERSEY:

In the year 1935 the world was facing major problems. After the first world war Germany was is a major depression, the situation was chaotic. The Nuremberg Laws was signed by Hilter on Sept 15,1935 this was the beginning of the nightmare for European jews.

In the United States the depression spurred the implement of Social Welfare Programs. [to Quote a great American Michael Picini " A major Sin is to have the ability and desire to work and not be able to fine a job."] To meet the crises the President and congress passed the Work Progress Administration [WPA] the Public Works Administration [PWA] . These agencies build 8,000 parks,1,600 schools, 800 airports,3,300 storage dams, 78,000 bridges and 65,000 miles of roads . Employing 8 to 14 million worksers.

In 1935 Congress passed the Social Security Act, which President Roosevelt later called the "supreme achievement of his administration.

Because American was still the land of opportunity the following invention and Ideas were developed:

Fluorescent Lights [GE]
Gallup Poll
Kodachome Film 16 mm movie camera
Beer in a can [Kruger Beer N.J.]
BRA cup sizes [A-D]
Parking Meter [Oklahoma]
Roller Derby
Richter Scale [measure earthquakes]
Sulfa Drug [to combat Bacterial infection]

On December 1935 Bing Crosby Began work on NBC Radio Kraft Music Hall.

Great People born in 1935:
Morris E Nicholson [Entrepreneur owner of Apollo Paper Company .]

Woody Allen [U.S. filmmaker.]
Jim Dine [U.S. artist]
Phil Donahue [U.S. talk show host]
Geraldine Farraro [U.S. political leader]
A.J. Foyt [U.S. auto racer]
Hussein [Jordanian King]
Loretta Lynn [U.S. singer]
Luciano Pravarotti [Italian opera singer]
Elivs Presley [U.S. singer]

SEMPER FI

MARK NICHOLSON IN HIS OWN WORDS:

It's hard to imagine that I could add anything to what's already been said. I spoke at the 35 year celebration in 1993; I read the mountain of letters from well-wishers; I attended the retirement party in 2003 where Dad as celebrated and where he bid farewell to the business.

When I joined the company in 1991 Apollo had already taken on sort of mythical proportions. It had survived paper shortages, frivolous lawsuits, the recession in the 80's and most recently the Butler Paper debacle in Dallas. Even though I'd grown up with Apollo Paper almost as a second sibling, I felt like I was a spectator. I still feel like I missed out on so many events that made the company such a success story. When Dad sold the company to Landsberg in 2001, the ten years I'd been there seemed like they went so quickly.

As mentioned earlier, I had the honor of speaking at Dad's retirement party and still remember the words of praise and pats on the back for a career that had blessed so many lives and provided a living for scores and scores of families over the years. Yet in a way, it was like they were talking about someone else.

So what can I add that no one else has contributed? Just this: Dad overcame not simply a bunch of headaches during his days as leader of the company, but also adversity that in today's entitlement society would have put the average man "on the dole" or in an institution. Today we look for all the excuses as to why we can't. Dad looked at his past experiences as a challenge; something he would prove he could rise above. His life is proof that with God anything is possible. I don't even know how truly tough he had it, but I know he grew up with few role models, sparse resources, little training and pretty much just one person who truly believed in him and told him he could do it.

So even with all the accolades, I don't think many outside the family even realize how hard Dad had to work to make it all happen. I doubt anyone who worked for Apollo really appreciated what a wonderful opportunity they had been given when they had it, or what a price had been paid for them to be part of that organization.

As I've sat on the sidelines, in many ways, and sometimes wished I could have been more of an insider, I am grateful to have had a front row seat to Dad's life and work that really only a handful of people have shared.

I know that Mom and Dad are planning to title this book, "It Was Fun." And fun it certainly was. But I'd have called it "It's Still Fun." Because Dad is still at heart the same champion who took the paper business by storm almost 60 years ago. I'm so proud to be his boy and so grateful to have had the chance to watch and learn from him these 48 years.

JULIE NICHOLSON IN HER WORDS:

I doubt there's much that I could say about Apollo Paper that hasn't already been said, especially since my connection with the company was so brief. Mark and I began dating in early 2000 and just a year and a half later Apollo was sold.

But I have one sweet memory of the company and its employees. The sale was announced in September and Mark resigned later that month. Our wedding was scheduled to happen just three weeks after that. And even though Mark wasn't an employee anymore, the Apollo team got together and gave us a shower and a really generous gift certificate that funded a trip the next year to Washington DC for our first anniversary. Most of them came to the wedding. And I just remember thinking this was a great group of people and one I was sorry not to have gotten to know better. I know over the years Apollo touched lots of other lives as well. Thanks for the opportunity to share one of my memories.

It Was FUN!

LYNDA NICHOLSON SNIDER IN HER OWN WORDS:

The first word that comes to my mind when I think about my life with my Father is BLESSED. I am blessed that I was raised by a loving, caring, hard-working father. I am blessed today that our relationship has grown beyond being father and daughter to being great friends.

Throughout my life my dad has always impressed me with his BIG WORK ETHIC and his ability to have BIG FUN!! When I was a little girl, dad was constantly showing me the "better way to do that." Hence, his great ability to work smart. That has definitely rubbed off on me when I think about my impatience for incompetence.

His love for fun is contagious!! I guess when you learn to have fun with oranges and apples as Christmas gifts, you can be easily entertained. One of my best memories with dad was travelling to Augusta, Georgia to watch the Masters golf tournament. (I was 17 and more interested in working on my tan than watching golf!) However, it was a great opportunity to spend some time with my father before I went to college. Every day on the way to the tournament, Dad would drive our rental car as fast as he could over the railroad tracks and gleefully exclaim, "Rent car!! It's OK!!" He can make anything FUN!! Unfortunately, the weather was cold, and I did not get much color, but we did have fun buying sweats at Sears....

When I went to work at Apollo at the very green age of 23, I was ready to set the world on fire! Dad gave me lots of advice like, "Leave the office by eight a.m. every day," and "Make lots of calls." We made our fair share of calls together, too. Dad has a great ability to talk. Anyone who knows him knows that. We were making a cold call on Cummins Southern Plains in Arlington, Texas, on a guy named Don. We were there until 5:30 p.m. Customers even stayed after work to talk to Nick! We got all the business. I couldn't wait to make calls with Dad because his closing ratio was AWESOME!

I have since "retired" from Apollo to be a stay at home mom. PaPa lights up his grandchildrens' lives with his visits and smiles.

I can not write something about Dad without mentioning my wonderful mother. How great is it that mom still loves Dad so much after 52 years of marriage that she wrote a book to honor him? She has been a great partner and faithful prayer warrior!! I love you, Mom.

It is always so great to look down at my phone and see an incoming call from "Dad."

I love you so much, Dad, and I am so proud of you!!

TONY SNIDER: IN HIS OWN WORDS

There are certain people in life that leave a lasting impression. Nick is without a doubt on that list! To describe him as a colorful personality is an understatement. Nick came into my life almost 17 years ago when I started to woo his beautiful daughter. I remember his appraising eyes when I first met him and Beverly. I realized that I had an uphill climb to be considered worthy of his little girl. Lynda is of course the apple of Nick's eye and it was apparent that it was going to take some time for him to warm up to sharing her with me.

It struck me early on that if I ever had children, I would feel the exact same way. Fast forward 17 years and I find myself married to Nick's wonderful daughter and surrounded by three of the most fantastic children in the world. I now know exactly what was going through Nick's mind when Lynda and I first started our journey together.

As I walk down memory lane, there are lots of fun adventures and conversations I have had with my father in law. I could talk about him giving me some golf lessons since every one knows a Scotsman should be able to navigate a golf course. After it was apparent that I wasn't headed for a PGA tournament any time soon, we found common ground in our mutual love of the outdoors.

Before I knew it, I was looking out the window of Alaska Airlines headed for the Yakutat River in Alaska. That fishing trip was definitely a highlight in my relationship with Nick. We had a lot of time to talk and get to know each other while we were cleaning fish. Now that I think about it, I can't remember him cleaning many fish... another testament to Nick's persuasive abilities! As the years have passed, I have discovered that my bond with Nick has reached a level that few husbands reach with their father in law. We have had some fun times together and I look forward to many more.

I have had the benefit of great male role models in my life when it comes to making a living. My father, papa, granddad and Nick epitomize a dying breed of the hard working, unwavering, sweat equity, salt of the earth kind of men that can effectively lead their families and contribute to society at a high level. Wouldn't it be amazing to bottle that wisdom and experience!

Nick's work ethic has led him to have high expectations of those around him, which naturally elevates the commitment levels of his fellow workers. Nick, like my other role models, came from humble beginnings and through sheer will and determination made something of their lives.

There are a number of things that I respect and admire in Nick. I love his positive, upbeat attitude. So often, people allow their attitude to limit their enjoyment and success in life. Nick's attitude has proven to be one of his greatest assets. I appreciate his love of country and respect his commitment to the armed forces. Last but not least, I love to see him interact with his grandkids. It warms my heart to see him genuinely enjoy being with them and imparting some of the knowledge that has served him well. I know that he looks forward to watching them grow and mature.

And that is why after all this time, I call Nick Dad because he is so much more than just my father in law, he is my close friend as well. I am truly blessed to have Nick and Beverly in my life.

THE GRANDCHILDREN, LAURA, BLAKE AND KATY IN THEIR OWN WORDS:

"PAPA, YOU ARE THE GREATEST GRANDPA EVER. I LOVE SPENDING TIME WITH YOU. I'M SO BLESSED TO HAVE YOU AS MY GRANDFATHER. I LOVE YOU. XOXOXOXOXO" LAURA

"PAPA YOU ARE A WONDERFUL GRANDPA AND I LOVE YOU SO MUCH! COME TO CHARLOTTE SOON SO WE CAN PLAY BASKETBALL. I LOVE YOU." BLAKE

"PAPA YOU ARE THE BEST PAPA ANYONE COULD EVER, EVER, EVER ASK FOR! I LOVE YOU SO MUCH! I LOVE YOUR SENSE OF HUMOR AND HOW YOU BRING A SMILE TO EVERYONE'S FACE. YOU ARE AMAZING. LOVE YOU." KAY KAY

DR. SID (SONNY) NICHOLSON IN HIS OWN WORDS:

Morris E. Nicholson—my recollections of Uncle "Moe"

First it should be noted that Uncle Moe possesses certain qualities that can be neither bought, sold nor taught. First is the gift of gab of which Moe is an expert, he seldom is caught at a loss for words, and can talk on a broad range of subjects. Secondly is an innate ability to make people almost instantly like him. He could come up to someone, insult them to their face and five minutes later the guy would be buying Moe a drink. Third is his ability to sell almost anyone something. I sincerely believe he could sell birth control pills to Nuns, pork chops to Jews, and set up a successful car dealership in the heart of Amish country. He is also generous and willing to help others.

Finally, he possesses LUCK. For some inexplicable reason the man has an inordinate share of plain old luck. How many people can let a blackjack pot ride for eight hands of play, not only win, but blackjack three times, and draw 21 once. He might have gone on a few more hands but I made him cash it in! Who usually caught the big Muskie or Northern? Moe of course, part skill, but a modicum of luck.

Because it has been 63 years since I came into being and was more or less thrust into the care of my uncles and aunt on the Nicholson side of my family, the memories are kind of foggy to say the least, especially considering the fact I was very young when I was born!

I spent a lot of time at Nanny and Paw paw's house when I was little and so I was kind of the little toy and almost a little brother to the Nicholson kids. Moe being the youngest, I guess I spent a good deal of time with him and his friends. My earliest memories were of Moe and his buddies playing basketball on the grass in the back yard. Even at that age I had a hard time figuring out how they played basketball without a paved surface, but most of the grass was worn off anyhow. I sat on the clothesline pole and watched them play. I actually remember going to a gymnasium and watching a game or practice a time or two.

Moe was a baseball player and I remember my grandfather Anthis said he taught Moe to throw a knuckle ball and I remember seeing Moe in a baseball uniform and pitching. He was a really good pitcher, but from what I understand not much of a hitter. For me it was the other way around.

Of course one of my strongest memories was of the time Moe was on the front porch shooting fireworks and I was a pretty little kid, but I guess I wanted to throw some lit fireworks too. Well, I probably got one with a short fast fuse and it went off in my hand, well I guess I commenced to hollering and Nanny came running out on the porch and tore Moe up over that like a banty hen protecting her chicks!

Another thing we did was listen to the St. Louis Cardinals radio broadcasts on the car radio. I'm not sure whose car it was, but we'd sit out there and listen and cheer for the Cards. It was a lot of fun and in some ways was better than going to a game, as in your mind's eye I could "see" the game and imagined the grass the stadium and all the players. That was a thing I continued to do (listen to the cardinal games) for many years and am still a diehard Cardinal fan.

Moe was kind of a skinny kid with kind of long combed back hair who worked in a clothing store for a while, and then for some reason unknown to me I was told he was going to join the Marine Corps. I didn't know why he would do such a thing, but I was told that he was going to be gone for a good while and I didn't like that at all! Much to my surprise a couple of months later he shows up bigger, a bur haircut and half of his front tooth missing (that's another story that only he can do justice to!). Then he was gone again.

My next recollection was that he had this cute girlfriend that talked funny from someplace called Iowa and that they were going to get married! Oh my gosh, this was going to be the marines all over again! I was losing my uncle to a girl!

We had a hiatus for a few years, I moved to Oklahoma, and Moe was busy building a business and family. We did go to a couple of Astros games, one against the Cardinals in the Dome. Cards won, Carlton pitched and the entire Cardinal infield was on the all star team that year.

Once after I got married, Linda and I came down to Houston for a visit and we watched Mark (can't remember if Lynda was born yet) while Moe and Beverly went somewhere. He was a cute little kid. Later on when we had kids, we would sometimes stay with Moe, Bev and their kids Mark and Lynda. Our kids were much younger, but had a good time with Mark and Lynda who played with them and had fun!

Starting in1994 we began a number of years of fishing adventures that began in Canada and later took us to Alaska. These were epic trips that featured lots of fish caught, lots of lies, endless strings of jokes and lots of fish dinners, pies, cakes and other good stuff.

The first year we went to Cedar Lake in N.W Ontario. To say that Moe had a dislike for the camp owner was to put it mildly. The guy followed Moe around waiting for him to throw down a cigarette butt, so he could tell him to not litter the camp. Needless to say, we didn't stay there the next year. Noteworthy on this trip was the continual barrage of jokes Moe came up with. Honestly, he told jokes for six solid days before he finally told one twice. We all laughed ourselves silly.

Also, because this was a small cabin, there were four beds all in the same room. Honest to Pete, Moe and my dad would immediately start snoring LOUD when they hit the sack and Scott and I would die laughing at all the racket those two guys made. After the sixth night of sleep deprivation, I was ready to sleep outside with the billion odd blood thirsty mosquitoes to escape the racket!

The second year found us in new digs at a camp on Cedar Lake owned by Roger and Carol. The cabin we had was huge, but was inhabited by a troop of mice, which we trapped. It was the night that the bat swooped low over Moe's head and sent him diving for cover that was priceless!

After a few years in Canada we switched to Alaska. Big fish and big country. Our destination was Yakutat where we had lots of adventures with big fish, awesome mountain scenery, crazy misfit guides, mean, sometimes clueless boat captains, fish eating bears, and at times incessant rains.

Our first trip was a mini disaster as it took us three days to get to our destination. The second night, stranded in Seattle with no clothes, tooth brushes or other essentials Moe raised all heck with Delta and they gave us a voucher for $50 each to buy some skivvies, socks, pants and etc. We went to Wal-Mart in a rented car, you'd have thought someone had given Moe a thousand bucks, he had a grand time in Wal-Mart- as we all did- buying our cheap but utilitarian stuff. We celebrated our good fortune by going down to the Seattle fish market area and having a delicious seafood dinner.

We finally got to Yakutat, and discovered that the thousands of salmon we saw, but were unable to catch. Finally, by chance we ran across some Germans fishing in a hole and although the spoke little English, Moe struck up enough of a conversation to gets the word "sinking" from them. We hung around till they left, got their spot and proceeded to catch so many salmon that we couldn't lift the stringer. From that point on, we slayed them in the river.

We went halibut fishing with a guy named Sparky (one of many in a long line of unusual characters). After about two hours of fishing, out from below deck comes this disheveled looking woman, we figured she was Sparky's bed warmer or maid or something. Other halibut guides included a guy who was Brian Piccolo's cousin, another guy who looked like he'd just spent the previous night smoking pot.

The most famous of all our guides was Frank Devereaux, misplaced Louisianan, ex sniper, and a guy who really got pissed off if you missed a strike on a halibut bite. Frank knew his stuff and could guide on the river for salmon and could catch a sockeye when they were running on about every cast. He taught us all a lot about fishing, despite his surly exterior; he did want to make you a better fisherman. Moe of course, invited him to our cabin for dinner on several occasions. Probably one of the more interesting characters we ever ran across. As we went back over the years we got to know some of the people in town and actually looked forward to going back and catching up on who got sick, what changes might have occurred since the previous year.

At the Situk R. there was a section of the river called the old man's hole and you had to be 60 to fish there, so I didn't qualify. One day my son and I were fishing upriver and I could see Moe and my dad downriver, all of a sudden my dad goes down in the river! Here comes Moe dragging him out and helping him up. From a few hundred yards upstream it was kind of like a silent Keystone Cops movie.

Another time we were all about in the same positions stream wise and I looked downstream and nobody was there. Then I saw Moe peeking around some brush looking toward Scott and I. I thought there might be some trouble, so I got Scott and we went back down stream to see if everything was ok. When we got there Moe proceeded to tell us in a most animated fashion that the bear that had harassed Scott and me earlier had come over the river bank opposite them and proceeded to try to get their fish. At this point in he related that my crazy father had tried to scare off the fish by beating a tin pan on a boat. It didn't work and they beat a hasty retreat to the safety of our vehicle.

At this point he said that I (I was carrying a .44 mag pistol) should come and guard them while they fished!   We went out on the end of the gravel bar and two minutes later here comes the bear.   OH SH..!   Out comes the .44! Fortunately the bear wasn't in a mood to take on four of us, and after growling, batting at some tree limbs and looking in some abandoned boats, ambled off to do whatever nuisance bears do.

Another time we went on a float down the Situk, and following a full day on the river, at dinner my dad keeled over at the dinner table!   Fortunately he survived, but he gave us all a moment or two of excitement.

Now, Moe was an excellent fish filleter, mind you I never saw him clean a fish, but he did offer excellent advice on the proper way to do it.   Following one day of a really big catch, Scott and I were filleting and packaging the catch for freezing.   The old men lost interest in our labors after an hour or so and wandered off.   About an hour later Moe shows up freshly bathed and sipping on a Crown and 7 up. At that point we had been fishing and cleaning fish for most of the day and tiredness was setting in. Anyhow, Moe said "What are you going to cook for dinner?" At that point I implied that you don't ask a tired man covered in fish slime and blood and holding a large sharp knife a question like that, and that he was going to buy something at the restaurant by the cabins for dinner.   He did.

One final episode I'll mention occurred on 9 mile bridge.   Moe was fishing in the hole below the bridge, as we all were, so up drives a car and two characters get out, one with a fishing rod and the other one carrying a trident kind of a gig.   Both of them were drunk and pretty soon the chubby one, walking around in his underwear throws the other guy off the bridge!   That unleashed a good cussing from the throw-ee (he lost his glasses in the river) at the thrower.

Well, a few minutes later Moe hooks a big king salmon (25-30-lbs.)And the fish takes off downriver and strips most of Moe's line off his reel and he's like, oh crap what now?   The chubby guy in his skivvies volunteers his services, Cajun man to the rescue!   He dives off the bridge in his under drawers, barefooted, and drunk, gig in hand to tame the monster fish!   A few minutes later here he comes, wet skivvies clinging to his torso (a scary sight!), fish on gig!   We gave the fish to him because it was illegal to keep kings that far up the river and we didn't have a king license anyhow.   Didn't make any difference to a couple of drunk guys, they threw it in their car trunk and took off!

These are but a few of the incidents I can remember and could actually reveal!   Suffice it to say our fishing adventures have been funny, fun times that are priceless memories!   Moe was a big part of the fun we all had together!

Now, Moe was an excellent fish filleter, mind you I never saw him clean a fish, but he did offer excellent advice on the proper way to do it. Following one day of a really big catch, Scott and I were filleting and packaging the catch for freezing. The old men lost interest in our labors after an hour or so and wandered off. About an hour later Moe shows up freshly bathed and sipping on a Crown and 7 up. At that point we had been fishing and cleaning fish for most of the day and tiredness was setting in. Anyhow, Moe said "What are you going to cook for dinner?" At that point I implied that you don't ask a tired man covered in fish slime and blood and holding a large sharp knife a question like that, and that he was going to buy something at the restaurant by the cabins for dinner. He did.

One final episode I'll mention occurred on 9 mile bridge. Moe was fishing in the hole below the bridge, as we all were, so up drives a car and two characters get out, one with a fishing rod and the other one carrying a trident kind of a gig. Both of them were drunk and pretty soon the chubby one, walking around in his underwear throws the other guy off the bridge! That unleashed a good cussing from the throw-ee (he lost his glasses in the river) at the thrower. Well, a few minutes later Moe hooks a big king salmon (25-30-lbs.)And the fish takes off downriver and strips most of Moe's line off his reel and he's like, oh crap what now? The chubby guy in his skivvies volunteers his services, Cajun man to the rescue! He dives off the bridge in his under drawers, barefooted, and drunk, gig in hand to tame the monster fish! A few minutes later here he comes, wet skivvies clinging to his torso (a scary sight!), fish on gig! We gave the fish to him because it was illegal to keep kings that far up the river and we didn't have a king license anyhow. Didn't make any difference to a couple of drunk guys, they threw it in their car trunk and took off!

These are but a few of the incidents I can remember and could actually reveal! Suffice it to say our fishing adventures have been funny, fun times that are priceless memories! Moe was a big part of the fun we all had together!

It Was FUN!

GREG RAINDL, VICE PRESIDENT AND CFO OF APOLLO PAPER COMPANIES IN HIS OWN WORDS:

I had the pleasure of working with Nick for 12 years. He is truly a special person. By profession Nick is a salesperson. Everyone has heard the saying that a good salesperson could sell ice to Eskimos. This man could not only close the sale, but would show them how to use it. Nick has an uncanny talent of remembering the smallest detail about a sale that occurred 30 years ago and is tenacious in his approach; he refuses to take no for an answer.

While selling is his first passion, Nick was also one of the founders and subsequently sole owner of Apollo Paper Company. Working with him could be both rewarding and frustrating. Because of his affinity toward sales, Nick would spend countless hours with the sales force training and counseling them in all facets of business. He especially gravitated to the rookies to make sure they understood what was expected. Nick could chastise a sales person one minute and hug them the next. While he is a tough ex-marine, at heart he's an old softy. Time spent on things that did not interest him was kept to a minimum. Accounting and financial matters were addressed only as a last resort.

Nick's philosophy of business is simple, work hard but have a good time. He demands loyalty and honesty from people he works with and gives the same in return. I remember turning in an expense report that had a receipt from a Mexican restaurant in San Antonio instead of a receipt from a local Mexican restaurant. Nick saw this immediately and chastised me for trying to get reimbursed for personal expenses. Needless to say, I was very careful in preparing my expense reports in the future.

Nick steadfastly refused to enter the computer age, but he recognized the benefits. In 1995 several of the management group were involved in a computer hardware and software conversion. As usual the conversion did not go according to plan and the hours required to get operational were enormous. Once the conversion was complete, Nick was so appreciative of the effort that he sent the key personnel on expense paid vacations.

Nick also believed in hiring the best available person for the job. He was able to assemble a dedicated and very successful team that grew Apollo Paper into one of the premier paper and packaging product companies in Texas. Nick always said that he wanted to hire people smarter than him. What Nick lacked in formal education he made up with good old fashioned common sense and hard work.

In 2001, after the sale of Apollo Paper, the new owners gave Nick a Blackberry. He promptly gave it to the receptionist and told her to call him if they needed anything. That Blackberry never saw the light of day.

Nick's most amazing personality trait is his ability to vanish at will. He could simply disappear without a trace. His magical powers were displayed at the most inopportune times. On numerous occasions, you could be meeting with Nick on a business matter, go to your office to get some information and return to find Nick gone.

It Was FUN!

NEIL BURNS, REGIONAL OPERATIONS MANAGER, KENT H LANDSBUR CORP, IN HIS OWN WORDS:

RETIREMENT SPEECH FOR NICK

I HAVE WORKED WITH AND KNOWN NICK FOR CLOSE TO 19 YEARS. I STARTED AS A TRUCK DRIVER. I AM CURRENTLY THE OPERATIONS MANAGER OF OUR DALLAS DIVISION. THANKS FOR CREATING A COMPANY WHERE THIS IS POSSIBLE NICK.

I HAVE A COUPLE OF STORIES TO SHARE WITH YOU, I HAD BEEN WITH THE COMPANY A COUPLE OF WEEKS AND WAS ROUTING MY TICKETS IN THE MORNING ONE DAY IN HOUSTON. NICK CAME BY AND SAID GOOD MORNING. I KNEW WHO HE WAS AND REPLIED "GOOD MORNING" MR. NICHOLSON. HE TURNED AND "WHAT DID YOU SAY"? I THOUGHT, "BOY YOU DID IT NOW". HE SAID "CALL ME NICK. I CAME FROM WHERE YOU ARE". I THOUGHT TO MYSELF, HERE IS THIS GUY WITH ALL THIS, HAS BUILT UP THIS GREAT COMPANY FROM SCRATCH AND IS SO DOWN TO EARTH. I WAS IMPRESSED AND WENT OUT AND MADE DELIVERIES LIKE THERE WAS NO TOMORROW.

YEARS LATER, I WAS OUR WAREHOUSE MANAGER IN DALLAS. WALT HAD RECENTLY HIRE LINDA (NICK'S DAUGHTER) AS A SALESREP. NICK CAME UP TO RIDE WITH HER AND NEEDED A NAVIGATOR IN DALLAS. I RODE WITH NICK AND LINDA AND MADE SALES CALLS WITH THEM FOR THE DAY. AT EACH ACCOUNT WE CALLED ON, I NOTICED THAT NICK ALWAYS KNEW JUST THE RIGHT THING TO SAY. WHETHER WE TALKING TO AN OLD COWBOY OR WE WERE TALKING TO A POLISHED BUSINESS PROFESSIONAL, HE KNEW HOW TO CUT RIGHT THROUGH AND PUT THEM AT EASE. HE DID THIS EFFORTLESSLY. I THOUGHT "MAN, HOW DOES HE KNOW HOW TO DO THIS"? I WAS AGAIN IMPRESSED.

I HAVE KNOWN A LOT A REALLY GOOD PEOPLE AND HAVE BEEN INFLUENCED BY A LOT OF THEM OVER THE YEARS. NICK IS ONE OF THE PEOPLE AT THE TOP OF THIS LIST. THANK YOU NICK FOR SHARING WITH ME YOUR LIFE AND ACCOMPLISHMENTS AND ALLOWING ME TO PARTAKE IN YOUR GOODNESS. I WILL FOREVER BE INDEBTED TO YOU AND NEVER LET YOU DOWN.

Neil Burns

DAN E. PICINI, CEO, DURATEST CORPORATION OF NEW JERSEY, IN HIS OWN WORDS:

Who is Morris E. Nicholson? He is my friend Nick. Nick and I became neighbors by location and friends by choice. I have been in business for over 30 years and met people in many businesses and countries. A wise man once wrote, life is a sieve which our acquaintances pass through. Those who are too big to pass through the sieve become our friends. . .

Nick is BIG IN MIND AND HEART. Dr. A. Athos (Harvard Professor) in his book "Our Changing World" separates business smarts into two categories: 1) Abstract smarts (academic) and 2) Experience smarts. He concludes that abstract smarts has hurt many businesses. Experience smarts builds businesses and provides opportunities.

Nick used his experience smarts to build a profitable and on-going business for him, his customers and employees at Apollo Paper Company. This was done by setting a MISSION, STRATEGIES and IMPLEMENTING each step. In this way he provided the best service for his customers.

Nick and I have shared many moments reviewing facts and ideas that would not only help business, but also our government. Nick is a born leader he honed his leadership skills in the Marine Corps. He exemplifies "Semper Fidelis" always faithful as: a son, brother, Marine, husband, father, grandfather, employer, Christian and my friend.

He is big in heart always helping many people through his Christian beliefs. Now retired, he is helping others build a new business. Every man must have a champion who believes in him and his cause. Nick's champion is his wife Beverly who also has a big heart in helping people.

I am thankful that both are my friends.

Sealed Air Corporation

TEN OLD SHERMAN TURNPIKE / DANBURY, CONNECTICUT 06810 (203) 791-3500 / FAX 791-3618

January 15, 2004

Dear Nick,

I am sorry I could not be with you Saturday, January 17th to acknowledge such a special occasion sharing memories with you and being with your family, friends and business associates.

Sometime before 1970, I believe you shared a dream with Beverley by gathering enough courage and asked her to risk everything. "We're going to put everything on the line." "I want to take a chance" You had a dream knowing exactly where you wanted to go and how to get there. When you and Joe started Apollo Paper, both of you were defying the percentages and conventional wisdom. I think all of us would agree in today's world, without the investment of millions of dollars, the odds of failure are good. To be sure, it was a long, often tough journey that you set out on, but, you triumphantly achieved your goals.

Today you are a super-successful businessman and well known throughout the paper industry. The price you have paid is hard work and dedication. Your rewards are influence, prestige and respect. I remember you often would tell me " I hit the ground running early in the morning" The difference between you and others is there are so many folks who get up and really don't know what to do and what they have to do. You knew exactly what to do. You would say, "If you look at it from the customer point of view, you usually wind up doing the right thing." Success is measured by one victory at a time. Obviously, you like to win and win you did. Over the years, you passionately nourished Apollo's growth, which became stronger and stronger. What is your secret?

I think you have many God-given gifts some of which is your ability to recognize the skills managing risk. In addition, I always have felt your best gift is the unique ability to find highly qualified people. You are successful and Apollo Paper is successful in part, because of the outstanding men and women recognizing you. What you did is offer a forum challenging this group to grow and build on their natural strengths by pulling together to make it happen on a day-to-day basis. You could never accomplish your dream without the importance of recruiting, developing, and retaining outstanding talent. You also recognized You had to eliminate much of the ' they' and 'we'   by creating a team among suppliers, corporate representatives and to recruit, develop, deploy, and retain human talent by blending into a truly outstanding Apollo team.   You cannot build a great team without great players. That is a fact.

Your Mom's memory is always with you and I think she would tell you, "If you work hard and you're honest, good things are going to happen you." She is right. I think she taught you family is your roots and the absolute base of life. Business is second.

Nick, I think you probably married over your head! You asked Beverley to risk it all. Through thick and thin, good decisions and bad decisions, good times and bad times she stood by her man. She was there and she believed in you. She paid the price knowing Dad was going to miss some ball games, maybe some school functions or other important life events while you developed Apollo. Beverley believed in you and your dream. I think you will agree many of your achievements are based upon the strong foundations set by your partner. So you and Beverley go celebrate your retirement knowing your legacy is a testament to the commitment and high standards you set in 1970. Frankly, Apollo Paper will be apart of Houston's fabric for many, many years to come...

I wish you a wonderful retirement.

Sincerely,

Joe Winston

JEFF SMALLWOOD, CITY SPECIALTY SALES DIRECTOR, NORTH AMERICA, NIKE CORPORATION, IN HIS OWN WORDS:

After playing golf at Deerwood CC one afternoon, as usual, we all go into the locker room for a cold beverage or two or three. . . While sitting at one of the tables Nick mentioned playing gin rummy. He said, "Jeff and me will play anyone in here for a dollar a point." I had never played gin before, so I didn't know exactly what a dollar a point meant.

A few seconds later some people within our golf group headed our way. The opportunity to play someone who had been drinking and someone who didn't know how to play was an opportunity too good to pass up. One of the bag boys was helping me, but it didn't take long for me to realize my partner needed a little help as well. Nick is holding gin in his hand. One of our opponents yells "gin" and goes down. Nick looked at his cards, we added them up and all the other gets is 25 points.

"We'll get them in the next game Pods, let's turn one more!" At this point I didn't know where we stood financially, so my Friendship and Loyalty went with it. After the second game which entailed a few more drinks, we totaled up the losses. Nick and I lost a bundle; the best gin lessons money could buy!

We had two groups playing golf all day, which usually involves a lot of trash talking, gambling and drinking. I'm not exactly sure how much had been said, lost or drank after playing 36 holes, but it's safe to say a lot. After sitting in the locker room settling everything up, I decided it would be a good idea to drive Nick home.

I followed him out to his car. He was opening the door and I said I'll drive you home. He didn't like the idea and playfully backed up with his fists up. He said, "watch this hand" which was above his head and held the keys. It was dark and as I reached for the keys the other hand hit me right in the groin. It hurt like hell. I grabbed Nick with both hands and said, "get in on the other side." He walked around and got in. As we started to pull out of the parking lot he leaned over and said, "I know you love me."

We've had a lot of good times over the years and I consider Nick a good friend. He would always talk about Bev and the kids and now he talks about the grandkids. We'd sit and talk about business, how he got started and how much he loved to work every day. I've tried to implement some of the things I learned from Nick in my own career. He has many personal qualities I respect and admire. He is loyal, generous, caring, competitive, humble, kind and never too busy to help in any way he can.